LITTLE TRAINS OF BRITAIN

JH

LITTLE TRAINS
OF BRITAIN

JOHN TIMPSON

PHOTOGRAPHY BY
ALAIN LE GARSMEUR

ADDITIONAL TEXT BY CHRIS AWDRY

HarperCollins*Publishers*

First published in 1992 by HarperCollins Publishers London

Main text © John Timpson 1992
Feature photography © Alain Le Garsmeur 1992
Maps, supporting text and additional photography © Julian Holland
Publishing 1992

The Author asserts the moral right to be identified as the author of this
work

A CIP catalogue record for this book is available from the British Library

ISBN 0 00 218425 7

Designed and conceived by Julian Holland Publishing Ltd

Typesetting by Minster Typesetters/PCS Typesetting
Cartography by Gecko Ltd

Printed and bound in Hong Kong

Supporting text and additional photography acknowledgments

Julian Holland Publishing Ltd would like to express special thanks to
Chris Awdry who supplied the supporting text and to the following
individuals who helped to supply that information:

Mr D Allen, Mr A B Beard, Dr T M Bell, Mr N Bowman, Mr J Brattey, Lord
Braybrooke, Mr D J Burgess, Caroline Butler, Mr F Crawley, Mr G Ellis, Lt
Cdr R W Francis, Mrs S G Gardner, Mr D J Guy, Mike and Liz Hallett, Mr
R Hardiman, Mr P J Hart, Mr A Ireland, Philippa Knowlson, Mr K L
Lewis, Lord O'Neill, Mr D O Roberts, Mr J B Southern, Mr G Stroud, Mrs
R Sutton, Mr R S Taylor, Mr A Turner, Richard Wall, Mr B Yarborough.

We would also like to thank the following individuals for supplying the
additional photography for pages 165–192:

Chris Awdry, Diana Awdry, Ron Bagley, Tony Beard, James Brattey,
Graeme Ellis, Redmond Gallagher, Julian Holland, Alastair Ireland,
Michael McKay, D T Stephenson, R S Taylor and Total Publishing Ltd.

Contents

Foreword

FIRST, a confession. I have never, ever wanted to drive a steam engine. Other trains, maybe. An Inter-City wouldn't be too bad – I quite fancy sitting there in splendid isolation behind the big glass windows, Lord of the Rails. I even see myself in the driver's cab of a Tube train on the London Underground, watching the rush-hour crowds as they struggle and heave to get on board before the doors close, then taking the curves and points at breakneck speed to ensure their maximum discomfort. Yes, I can see the job satisfaction in that.

But somehow I never yearned to man the footplate of a steam locomotive. As a small boy it always struck me as a most uncongenial job, exposed to the elements, dirty and draughty, surrounded by steam and smoke. And there was all that physical effort of shovelling coal and turning wheels and pulling levers.

The engines themselves did have an attraction. I remember leaning over a footbridge in Harrow on my way to school each morning to watch an early express hurtle underneath me on its way to Scotland, a magnificent roaring monster sending a great plume of smoke billowing up around me, leaving me gasping and blinking and speckled with soot, but curiously exhilarated, as if for a moment I had disappeared inside a volcano. And there was the moment of wonder one morning when I saw the Coronation Scot, streamlined and gleaming, with hardly a wisp emerging from where its funnel ought to be.

Later, living in Norfolk in the 'Fifties, I got to know the little engines that puffed around the branch lines, past the flintstone cottages and the splendid medieval churches and the rolling fields of barley and beet. Then the diesel railcars took over, and finally Beeching closed the lot. At that stage I never expected to see a steam engine working again.

Yet in the past year I have seen more working engines than I ever dreamed still existed. I have been in the world of the narrow-gauge railways, a world of enormous enthusiasm and perseverance and enterprise, where steam still reigns supreme. But I discovered to my relief that my lack of ambition to work on the footplate was actually shared by a great many of the railway volunteers I met. There is a lot more to restoring and running a steam railway than driving the engines, and those who work the signals and staff the stations, who polish the brasswork and sweep out the sheds, who shovel the ballast and cut back the weeds, get just as much enjoyment and satisfaction as the drivers and firemen and guards.

The passengers quite enjoy themselves too...

When I entered this world I rather feared that every narrow-gauge railway might turn out to be much the same. I also expected the people who ran them to be distinctly odd. After all, I thought, what normal grown-up would want to dress up in an ex-British rail guard's uniform, or a greasy overall and a shiny black cap, and play trains?

I need not have worried on either count. Each railway has its own character, its own unique features, it own remarkable history. And although I did come across some slightly eccentric folk – thank goodness! – the vast majority of railway volunteers have their heads in the smoke-clouds but their feet firmly on the ground.

At the beginning I had only the faintest idea of how a steam locomotive worked. At the end, in spite of many patient attempts to educate me, I still wasn't too sure. But I did learn a lot about the railways where these engines operate, and the people who operate them. I learned that you don't need to be a railway buff to enjoy the stories behind the *Little Trains of Britain*; they are as fascinating, and sometimes as astonishing, as anything you find in fiction. And I learned something of what motivates people of all ages and occupations, from all walks of life, to devote so much of their time and talents to bringing these lines back to life – though I did not discover until the end of the last chapter the simple word that explains it all.

No, I still don't want to drive a steam engine. But now I can understand why people do.

John Timpson, 1992

Opposite: 'Dolgoch' *with a down train at Quarry Siding Halt, Talyllyn Railway.*

Welshpool & Llanfair Light Railway

THE *Countess* puffed gently to a halt at Dolarddyn Crossing, and beside me on the footplate Tim Furber, the volunteer fireman, gave me a grin as he picked up a well-worn red flag. Normally he operates an ultra-modern signal-box on British Rail.

'We're very bucolic around here,' he explained, and clambered down onto the track. Behind us some of the passengers leaned out of the windows to watch, as he walked to the middle of the crossing and looked carefully up and down the tiny country lane.

I looked too. Indeed, we all looked. Apart from a few sheep in a nearby field and some cows on a distant hillside the Welsh countryside was devoid of life; the lane itself was manifestly deserted. Nonetheless, Tim solemnly held his flag aloft, and just to make quite sure, *The Countess* gave a warning whistle. Then we advanced cautiously across the lane, and as we came level with Tim he swung himself back on board. The operation had been successfully completed; it was the nearest thing we still have in Britain to the man who used to walk ahead of the engine with a red flag...

Del Curtis, the policeman from Ledbury who was driving *The Countess*, nodded approvingly and sounded the whistle again. Then Tim glanced at the sharp incline ahead, and picked up his shovel. 'Really,' he said cheerfully, 'what a silly place to build a railway!'

He was right, of course, as the people who built it soon found out. But when the Welshpool & Llanfair Light Railway was launched at the turn of the century it was an occasion of great rejoicing and jubilation. There had been a plan for the line to follow a more

'The Countess', pulling a Llanfair-bound train.

gently graded route from Llanfair to Llanymynech, further north, which would miss out Welshpool altogether. The idea was that, with the gentler gradients, a standard gauge line could be built to connect with the main line to Oswestry. But the Light Railway Commission held an enquiry in 1897 and came down in favour of a 2'6"-gauge line on the steeper, but shorter and cheaper route to Welshpool.

Welshpool was delighted. The church bells were rung all day, and no less a dignitary than Viscount Clive, son of the Earl of Powis, whose castle overlooks the town, cut the first sod. That was in 1901, and the line opened two years later.

So much for the good news. The bad news was that the railway cost more than twice the original estimate, and although much of it was contributed by the Treasury and local authorities, the company was never able to make money. It was not for lack of passengers – the trains were often crammed to capacity. But the company did not have the capital to buy more rolling-stock, and Cambrian Railways, which operated the line for them, was never even paid for the essential signalling equipment it installed. There was a boost during the First World War from the transport of timber, but in 1923 the ownership of the line, and its operation, were taken over by the Great Western Railway – who promptly started a bus service along the same route...

It did not need a Dr Beeching to bring about the next development. Passenger traffic ended on the Welshpool & Llanfair in 1931 and the line was turned over entirely to freight. It kept going during the 1939-

Right: 'The Countess' *passing* 'Sir Drefaldwyn' *as it approaches Llanfair.*

Welshpool & Llanfair Light Railway

The Station, Llanfair, Caereinion, Powys, SY21 0SF. Tel. (0938) 810441

Route: Llanfair Caereinion – Welshpool (Raven Square)
Distance: 8.5 miles
Gauge: 2 ft 6 in
Service: Daily mid Jul – early Sept; BH Easter – early Oct; Tue/Th mid Jun – mid Jul.

One of the first railways built under the 1896 Light Railways Act, this rural line opened for freight on 9 March 1903, officially on 4 April and to passengers on 6 April the same year. It has some of the steepest gradients on adhesion railways in Britain, and was built to carry general merchandise, coal, timber and livestock between farms in the Banwy valley and Welshpool, their market town. Trains ran through the back streets of the town to the standard gauge station, where there were interchange facilities. The W&L was worked by the Cambrian Railways Company, though

it remained independent until absorbed into the GWR in 1923. The last passenger train ran on 9 February 1931, but goods traffic continued and in 1948 the line became part of the nationalised British Railways. The last train ran on 3 November 1956. A preservation society was formed to save the line, and the first section re-opened to passengers on 6 April 1963. The line now ends on the west side of Welshpool. As well as the two original locomotives, *The Earl* and *The Countess*, the Society has locomotives from West Africa and the West Indies.

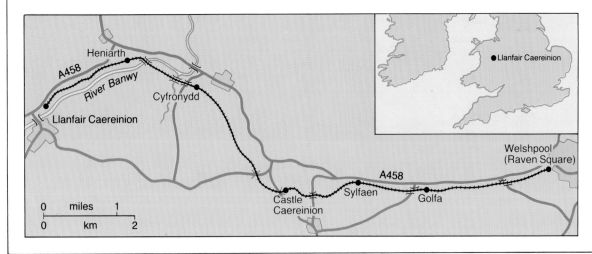

The little shunting engine 'Dougal' in Llanfair.

45 war, then goods traffic steadily declined. With nationalisation the line became part of British Railways in 1948, and it was not too long before some of the sidings were being taken up at Welshpool. The 'last train' ran in November, 1956, comprising nine coal wagons and two brake vans, packed with 150 enthusiasts who were determined that it would not be the last train after all.

It took four years to set up the Welshpool & Llanfair Light Railway Preservation Company, and another three for the first four-mile section of track to be re-opened to passenger traffic, between Llanfair and Castle Caereinion. Appropriately, it was re-launched by the Earl of Powis, descendant of the original sod-cutter.

But there was still much to be done. At the other end of the line the final section into Welshpool had been irretrievably lost – it had been excluded from the company's lease and the track was lifted. This meant the company had no proper terminus at the Welshpool end, and it had to make Llanfair its base. From a scenic point of view this was not a bad thing. Llanfair is a delightful little market town, perched on the hillside above the River Banwy, with the main road into mid-Wales now bypassing it so that its unhurried atmosphere has been restored. Its only obvious concession to the tourist industry is the sign over the venerable building in the town centre, which announces with an endearing brashness: TOWN HALL CHIPPY.

Between Llanfair and the river is a pleasant stroll through the Deri Woods, and helpful signs direct you to the Gorsedd Stones, remnants of a much earlier venue for visitors; this is where they still proclaim the Powys Eisteddfod. But in the main Llanfair is uncrowded by tourists and uncongested by traffic, altogether a more peaceful place than Welshpool from which to run a railway.

Having established itself at Llanfair Station the preservation society tackled the task of re-opening the rest of the line. Much of it between Castle Caereinion and Welshpool was completely overgrown; there were actually saplings growing between the rails on the

The ever-watchful eye of a railway guard at Welshpool Station.

Opposite: *Llanfair-bound 'The Countess' leaves Sylfaen Halt.*

mile-long Golfa incline, the steepest gradient of this length in Britain worked by conventional steam trains. To add to the problems, the bridge over the River Banwy was severely damaged by storms in the year after the first section to Castle Caereinion was opened, and it had to be closed again.

But railway enthusiasts are not daunted by a little matter like rebuilding a railway bridge over a wide, fast-flowing Welsh river. A national appeal was launched, the Army provided equipment and exper-tise, and while the work was going on, the company kept a little money coming in by running trainloads of sightseers and wellwishers from Llanfair Station as far as the bridge, to see what was happening. In August 1965, eight months after the bridge was damaged, the first passenger train crossed it safely, and they have been crossing it safely ever since.

There was still much work to be done, and it took many years of voluntary effort to do it. Castle Caereinion Station, which was as far as they'd got, may sound rather grand, but it is actually quite tiny, it is out of sight of the actual village, and there isn't any castle. There is just a 1907 signal-box (with no signals), a pleasant picnic place, and some splendid views of the mountains. To make the line at all viable, trains had to get through to Welshpool, nearly four miles further on.

By 1972 they had got as far as Sylfaen. It was only another mile, but at least the track adjoins the main road at this point, so it was a handy place to join the train. The toughest task, clearing the Golfa incline and creating a new station at Welshpool, still lay ahead. It was at this stage that the Manpower Services Commission came to the rescue, and the present general manager, Andy Carey, entered the picture.

In the mid-1970s Andy Carey was managing a freight-forwarding company at Birmingham Airport. He had been a volunteer helper on the Welshpool & Llanfair for years, and when the MSC offered to help he took on the job of supervising the work. By now the saplings had grown into fair-sized trees, and it must have been more like lumberjacking than line-clearing.

Collapsed culverts had to be rebuilt, road crossings re-laid, and the trackbed drained, covered with new ballast, and provided with 6,500 new sleepers.

Meanwhile at the site of the new Welshpool Station at Raven Square, on the outskirts of the town, a stream was diverted and the land drained, so a platform could be built and a signal-box erected. This was where the final re-opening ceremony took place in 1981, when the entire length of the line came into use again at last – and happily, it was again the Earl of Powis who performed it. Andy Carey, his supervisory duties for the MSC successfully completed, stayed on with the railway as assistant manager, looking after sales and publicity, and then as full-time manager.

It was his young assistant, David Moseley, who showed me round the engine sheds and the station buildings at Llanfair, and introduced me to other volunteers. I say 'other,' because although David is now a full-time employee he still does extra voluntary duties as well. On the day before I met him he had finished his official duties at about six o'clock – looking after the accounts and the office administration, running the booking office and the shop, answering telephone enquiries and working out the loco roster. In an emergency, incidentally, he puts his own name on the roster and drives the engine himself. Then at six he shut up shop, put on his overalls, and worked in the carriage shed for the next three hours, re-bushing one of the axles. In the world of little trains, I soon discovered, there are few demarcation lines when there is work to be done – and nobody watches the clock.

David works a seven-day week, five on the railway and two as a part-time insurance claims clerk. His parents hadn't expected him to do either when he went to college to learn business studies – though that has actually come in quite handy in the office at Llanfair Station. After leaving college he worked in the family hotel for four years, went on a catering course – and hated it. All this time he had been doing voluntary work on the railway; he first went there after finishing his O-levels, intending to stay the weekend, and arrived home six weeks later with arms-full of dirty washing.

'My parents had always encouraged me to do something practical, so I did.' David chuckled. 'They've never stopped complaining since – "you'll never make a living at it," they said, and of course they were perfectly right. But the beauty of this job is, there's always something interesting to be getting on with.'

He was going to have something particularly interesting to get on with later that day, in which I was involved as a passenger, but neither of us knew it at that stage...

The Welshpool & Llanfair has some 170 voluntary helpers, about a tenth of its total membership of supporters. I did meet one local Welshman, but most of them come from much further afield – Liverpool, Birmingham, London, the Home Counties. One entire family of volunteers comes up from Hampshire, father, mother, two sons, two daughters. And I met a businessman who drives sixty miles, sometimes to drive an engine but quite often just to help keep the track clear of vegetation. 'My wife says, why do I travel sixty miles to do gardening in Wales when I can step out of the back door and do it in my own garden? It's a difficult one to answer...'

Left: *The rural station of Cyfronydd.*

Right: *'Sir Drefaldwyn' built 1944, rebuilt 1957 in Austria, bound for Llanfair.*

I also met Dave Smith from New Zealand, an inveterate railway enthusiast, fortunately of independent means, who spends six months of each year in Britain, and five of those months at Llanfair. 'I looked at all the other narrow-gauge railways in Britain, but this one reminded me most of New Zealand. The hillsides, the valley, the river, the cows and sheep...'

So if he was so keen to be reminded of New Zealand, why bother to leave it? The answer was simple: there are no narrow-gauge steam railways in New Zealand. So he camps out at Llanfair Station, helps in the engine sheds, and spends much of his time cutting back hedges alongside the track. One day, maybe, he'll drive an engine, but he's not too bothered; he's working on a steam railway...

Dave was the only overseas volunteer on the Welshpool & Llanfair, but its engine and passenger stock is amazingly cosmopolitan for such a small railway, tucked away in the Welsh hills. The first thing you see at Llanfair Station is the massive Belgian loco built for use in Finland, now parked in the station entrance awaiting funds for restoration. In the engine shed I met *Joan*, formerly used to haul sugar cane in Antigua, and *Sir Drefaldwyn*, which in spite of its Welsh name was built in France, used by German military field railways in the last war, and later worked on Styrian Railways in Austria.

Little *Dougal* is not strictly foreign, just Scottish; it used to chunter around the Provan Gasworks in Glasgow before forsaking the rat-race to start a new career as a yard shunter at Llanfair. One of only two working engines to survive from the earliest days of the Welshpool & Llanfair is *The Countess*, ninety years old and still going strong – or as it turned out later that particular day, fairly strong...

The carriages come from distant parts too. Five are Austrian, rather splendid wood-panelled affairs with balconies on the end, and four were used in Sierra Leone, though admittedly they were built in Gloucester. They lack the fancy woodwork and the balconies of their Tyrollean neighbours, but they do have upholstered seats, so on most trains you can

choose between vintage elegance and modern comfort. Happily I did not have to make the decision; I was up front on the footplate with Del and Tim.

Even an Austrian wooden seat would have been more comfortable, because the cab of *The Countess* is a little cramped for three people, and it tosses about quite alarmingly at times. But it was considerably more exciting, especially when Tim needed more elbow-room to shovel coal. I had no idea I could be so acrobatic, but a shovelful of coal heading for an open fire-door can be a great incentive.

The fire has to be kept well stoked on the Welshpool & Llanfair because of the frequency and steepness of the gradients, but fortunately Tim was using some of the line's dwindling supply of Welsh steam coal. There is very little of it about these days, and David Moseley had waxed anything but lyrical over the Russian coal they were having to buy. 'The locos have to work hard on this line, and you need decent quality coal to produce enough heat. The Russian stuff lamentably

The line photographed from the end balcony of one of the Austrian-built wooden carriages.

Opposite: 'The Countess' *steaming up the 1 in 29 Golfa Bank.*

fails to do that – it just sits there and waves at you.' It was a story I heard repeated many times on other narrow-gauge railways – but it was only at Llanfair that they have on show in the office a lump of Russian 'coal' which actually has worm-holes in it...

On this trip, however, it was not coal that caused a problem, it was the Welsh equivalent of Network South-East's notorious 'leaves on the line'. Leaves only fall in the autumn, but on a track with steep gradients the same result can come from a fine, steady drizzle – and in Wales you can get a fine, steady drizzle all the year round. On this day we were let off lightly – it didn't start until the afternoon. Our morning run from Llanfair to Welshpool went entirely according to plan.

We crossed the Banwy on the re-built bridge, which looks quite alarming from the footplate because you can see down past the rails into the water. The new lattice girders didn't look nearly as reassuring as the one remaining stone pier. But the bridge is for trains, not pedestrians, and trains don't get vertigo. They can get the wobbles, though, and on the very sharp curves there's an extra rail to steady the wheels. Not that *The Countess* needed it; we took them very gently indeed, as we wound our way alongside the river and on to Sylfaen station. It is just a platform and a parking space, but Tim Furber surveyed it with some pride nonetheless. 'Would you believe,' he said, 'in the railway gazetteer, Sylfaen looks just the same size as Euston...'

We came to another crossing and he jumped off to wave his flag. There are six altogether, and one crossing is fitted with gates which Tim had to open, then the guard at the back of the train had to shut them after we'd gone through. It all adds up to a lot of stopping and starting, and Del Curtis commented wryly as we pulled up yet again: 'Cars are fine for bringing passengers for the railway, but they're a real nuisance on the railway itself.'

There is one exception to this routine, the Coppice Lane crossing, which the line approaches up a steep incline on each side. Trains are allowed to take it non-

Built 1902 by Beyer Peacock, Manchester, 'The Countess' stands at Welshpool Station.

Opposite: 'Sir Drefaldwyn' *is waved on through yet another level crossing.*

stop, giving several warning blasts on the whistle. Coppice Lane rarely has any traffic and this has never caused any problems, whereas there could be one, I gathered, if the engine had to re-start on the incline. On the way back I found out why...

But it was downhill all the way now, and we wriggled down the curves on the Golfa incline and arrived at Raven Square station fifty minutes after leaving Llanfair, bang on time. I climbed down a little shakily from *The Countess* – she really does bounce about quite skittishly for a ninety-year-old – thanked Del and Tim, and set off to savour the delights of Welshpool.

Thank goodness I arrived by train; the peak of the holiday season is not the best time to drive into Welshpool. It must enjoy, if that is the word, some of the heaviest traffic and the longest jams in the Borders. One guidebook very fairly likens it to a kind of Clapham Junction for motorists entering or leaving mid-Wales. It all builds up at the crossroads in the town centre, and if you pause there on the narrow pavement, attempting to read the plaque on what is now an estate agent's office, you are likely to have the seat of your pants removed by a passing lorry.

In case you don't care to chance it, I can tell you that it says the house was built by descendants of Roger Jones, who lived in the reign of Edward VI and was reputed to be the first Welsh Jones. It said a lot more too, but at that point my nerve cracked and I dived for cover. One day I must go back and find out what it meant...

Welshpool does have some quiet corners, and out of season I am sure it is delightful. It also has the Montgomery Canal, which has undergone a restoration programme quite as prolonged and arduous as the Welshpool & Llanfair. It has the additional bonus, however, of enjoying the personal interest of the Prince of Wales, who has visited it, says the brochure proudly, 'no less than three times'. This must give it, I thought, a more up-market social cachet than the railway, even with its support from the ever-present Earls of Powis. I found the railway had an answer to

that, when I got back to Llanfair; but in getting there, I discovered there was one field in which the canal definitely had the edge. It doesn't have steep inclines – and it doesn't get slippery in the rain...

It was raining when I got back to the station, about ten minutes before departure time. There was quite a crowd waiting, but no train, and this seemed sufficiently unusual to warrant a discreet enquiry. I learned there had been 'problems' getting up one of the steeper inclines, but the train was well on its way.

The crowd grew, the rain continued to fall. I cast a melancholy glance at the wooden stakes near the platform which marked the site of the new station building. By now, I trust, it will be erected, a Victorian station with all the trimmings, built in 1863 for Eardisley, on the old Hereford, Hay & Brecon Railway, and due to be transported to Welshpool in time for Easter 1992. It was costing £65,000, and I hoped my poundsworth of raffle tickets would help, but the bulk of it came from a legacy left by Stanley Keyse, who helped to form the preservation company and continued to support it until his death – and beyond.

But on that rainy day last August there was nothing to see but the stakes. We stood in the rain, displaying a stoic, even cheerful calm. It was a very British scene. But after all, nobody was in much of a rush; if we weren't getting wet on that platform, we'd be getting wet somewhere else.

About half-an-hour behind schedule, *The Countess* puffed into the station. I caught a glimpse of Del and Tim on the footplate, looking slightly fraught, and I was glad they hadn't had me to contend with as well. The passengers got off, seemingly unperturbed – at least they'd been out of the rain – and we piled on board. I made sure of a Sierra Leone padded seat, in case the journey took longer than scheduled. It was a wise move.

Del and Tim did a quick turnround, and we set off in fine style. It was the Golfa incline, one in 29 and very winding, which started the trouble. *The Countess* slowed a little, then slowed a little more – and stopped. Del walked past the window and had a deep

discussion with the guard, a normally cheerful character from south-east London who was spending his annual holiday working on the line. He was not looking quite so cheerful now.

I looked towards the engine and with some misgiving observed that Tim was filling a bottle with sand. Manifestly the sandboxes which were supposed to sprinkle sand on the rails just in front of *The Countess's* wheels were not functioning. Del returned to the footplate, Tim sprinkled energetically, and to universal relief the train moved forward. We all relaxed.

That was a mistake. At Sylfaen Station, where the line meets the main road, the stationmaster from Welshpool was waiting for us in his car – with a very large bucket of sand. David Moseley was there too

Opposite: *Castle Caereinion Station with its loop line, an important halfway stop.*

Full steam ahead out of Welshpool Station for 'The Countess'.

from Llanfair, clutching a red flag. Del and Tim and the distinctly uncheerful guard joined them in lengthy conclave. Just like a summit talk, I thought – then realised that was exactly what it was. The summit at Coppice Lane lay ahead of us, with that steep gradient up to the crossing. Were we going to have a crack at it, or was it going to be a long hike to Llanfair?

The meeting broke up. Tim took the bucket of sand, he and Del returned to *The Countess*, David and the stationmaster returned to their cars, the guard returned to his van. We heard an optimistic blast on the whistle, and we were off. As they say on the Matterhorn, we were going for the summit.

We didn't make it. Not at the first go, anyway. *The Countess* slowed again, and slowed, and stopped. This must be the end.

We passengers speculated on our next move. One school was in favour of walking back to Sylfaen and hitching a lift to Welshpool, another suggested driving a car along the track ahead of *The Countess*, tossing sand out of the rear windows. I recalled that our engine-driver was actually a policeman; if all else failed, perhaps he could commandeer a passing coach...

We heard *The Countess* making determined noises, and everyone rushed to the windows. There was Tim with his bucket, sprinkling the rails ahead of the engine. Del sounded the whistle and the train moved forward a foot, then paused, and started rolling backwards. Welshpool, I thought, here we come.

But this must have been a ploy to put sand on the wheels, so they could get a better initial grip when combined with fresh sand that Tim was pouring on the track. We were going forward now, very slowly but quite surely, with Tim sprinkling sand as if there were no tomorrow. All along the train I could see people leaning out the windows, willing *The Countess* on – and a memory of that old gramophone record came back to me from my youth:

'I...think...I...can, I..think..I..can, I think I can, I-think-I-can, I..know..I..can, I know I can, I-*KNOW*-I-Can...'

And she could.

At the Coppice Lane crossing David Moseley was waiting for us, waving his red flag in encouragement. He was at the next crossing too, and the one after that, waving his flag at the traffic so *The Countess* had a clear run, picking up a minute here and a minute there. It is no mean feat, I gather, to leap-frog a train to the crossings along these winding Welsh lanes, but he was always there ahead of us.

I caught his eye as we sailed past him on the final crossing, and he beamed up at me from the roadway. 'All part of the job!' he yelled. And he was there to receive us at Llanfair Station, and to apologise to passengers who in fact were in excellent heart, and indeed full of congratulations for the way he and Del and Tim had responded to the crisis. We had had an adventure above and beyond what was promised in the brochure, and so far as I know nobody was any the worse.

Some lessons were learned that day, and I doubt it has happened again. In some ways, more's the pity, because restoring and operating a narrow-gauge steam railway is fraught with such problems, and half the fun must be solving them. No doubt it is gratifying to achieve perfection, but having achieved it and maintained it for a while, for the pioneering railway volunteer – what next?

I bade my farewells and left the station, but before driving off I had a look at the new footbridge which has been built across the River Branwy to provide a short cut from the station to the town. It is a very handsome bridge, with a very handsome plaque. And here was the final accolade, which put the Welshpool & Llanfair on an equal social footing with the Montgomery Canal. The bridge had had a formal opening ceremony, I read, but the opener was not one of the ubiquitous Earls of Powis.

It was His Royal Highness the Prince of Wales.

Right: 'Sir Drefaldwyn' *making its way through the lush vale of Meifod.*

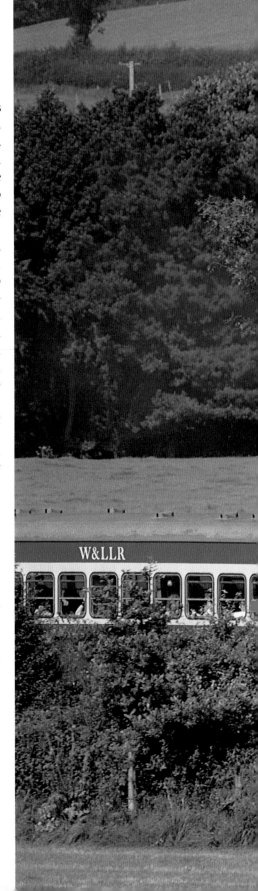

Ravenglass & Eskdale Railway

WHEN I first encountered the Controller of the Ravenglass & Eskdale Light Railway he was washing out the ladies' toilet on Ravenglass Station with a bucket and mop. I did not appreciate who he was at the time; let's face it, the Fat Controller of sacred memory was rarely associated with buckets and mops, let alone a ladies' lavatory. When I next met Graham Withers, however, it was in more Controller-like surroundings, in front of a console in the signal-box, and he was engaged in more Controller-like duties – drawing lines on a time-and-distance graph, radio-ing instructions to the drivers up the line, filling in sheets for those yet to leave, checking the positions of the trains.

But light railways being what they are, he had other matters to cope with too. Our conversation was frequently suspended while he took a telephone booking for a party of schoolchildren, or left his electronic gadgetry to pull some of the oldfashioned signal levers next door, or used the public address system to tell passengers on Platform Three to all-change please. Booking clerk, signalman, station announcer, and if necessary lavatory attendant; they all come into the job description. It might not be acceptable to a signal-man on British Rail – which is maybe why Graham stopped being one...

He is just one of the train enthusiasts who gave up more orthodox jobs to come to this remote and rather unfashionable corner of the Lake District and spend their working lives, and much of their spare time, on the Ravenglass & Eskdale. One or two of the drivers have been there for twenty years; Graham and the general manager, Douglas Ferreira, go back much

'Northern Rock' coming to a halt at Muncaster Mill Station.

further, to the days when the line was put up for sale by the granite company which owned it, with the threat that if no reasonable bid was made, it would be split up into sixty lots and sold piecemeal – the ultimate ignominy.

This was not the first crisis in the history of 't' la'l Ratty', as the locals call it – an engineer called Ratcliff built it, and it has been 'the little Ratty' ever since. By all the rules of business and logic it should have disappeared long ago. Its fortunes have had as many ups and downs as the track does itself, on its progress up the Esk Valley. Ratcliff took the cheapest and easiest route, to save the shareholders the expense of digging cuttings and building embankments, so from the driver's cab the line ahead can be reminiscent of a fairground rollercoaster, albeit with gentler gradients. The rises and falls in its financial history have been even more dramatic...

Whitehaven Iron Mines Ltd set up a railway company nearly 120 years ago to build a three-foot gauge line which would carry ore from its mines up in the hills at Boot to the main line at Ravenglass, seven miles down the valley. It opened in 1875, and there seemed no reason why it should not keep running

Right: 'Northern Rock' *coming to a halt at Eskdale Green Station.*

Ravenglass & Eskdale Railway

Ravenglass Station, Ravenglass, Cumbria, CA18 1SW. Tel. (06577) 226

Route: Ravenglass – Eskdale, nr Boot
Distance: 7 miles
Gauge: 15 in
Service: Daily April – 1 Nov, 26 Dec – 1 Jan; some w/e Nov, Feb.

To the surprise of many, this little line is now well past its Centenary, having been opened in 1878. When the haematite (iron ore) mines on which it depended closed in the early 1920s its future hung in the balance until Bassett-Lowke, in 1927, converted the railway from its original 3-foot gauge to one of 15 inches. It carried passengers as well as serving a stone quarry, but when, in the early '50s the quarry also closed, its future once again became uncertain. In 1958 it was up for sale. There were, at first, no takers, and it was then decided to sell the railway in separate lots at auction. An appeal to save the line as a whole was launched,

but not until the last weeks before the sale (in Gosforth Village Hall, in 1962) did funds begin to flow to an extent that would allow a bid to be made. This was successful, a Preservation Society was formed, and an ever-increasing stream of visitors and supporters has justified this action ever since. Much progress has now been made, and the Company is now exporting to Japan steam engines built in its Ravenglass workshops. The line has been a pioneer in this country of train control by radio, and a derivation of the system developed here is now used by BR.

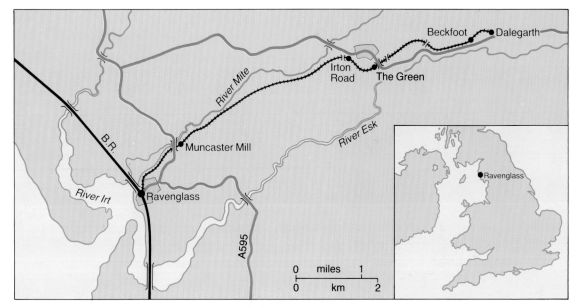

Last minute oil check on 'River Mite'.

successfully until there was no more ore to carry. A year later, however, it was decided to expand its activities to take passengers as well, and the decision proved disastrous. People can be more expensive to carry than lumps of rock, and there may have been no great demand to travel to Boot, to boot.

Two years after the line opened the railway company went bankrupt, and Ratty could have entered the record books as the shortest-lived line in railway history. Instead it has achieved a very different record, as the oldest narrow-gauge railway in England – but only after a series of closure dramas, and this was the first. The mining company still needed the railway to carry its ore, so instead of being closed it was put in the hands of a Receiver, who kept it going. So far, so good. But five years later the mining company itself closed down, and Ratty's main source of income disappeared.

How it kept going after that is something of a mystery. The official handbook says it existed on scraps of local traffic, a bit of granite quarrying and a few tourists 'and struggled on surprisingly for another 27 years'. It could hardly have spent a penny on maintenance or repairs, and I wouldn't have fancied risking a ride on the Ravenglass & Eskdale when it eventually gave up the struggle in 1908.

Another closure drama, and another reprieve. The Eskdale Railway Company was formed, and the line carried granite and iron ore – but wisely, no passengers – for a few more years. Then the final blow: the mines at Boot were flooded out, the iron ore business died, and so far as Little Ratty was concerned, Boot became, as it were, Boot Hill. In 1913 the line expired.

Nobody at that time could have believed that it would ever function again. For two years it lay derelict. Then over the hill came a knight in shining armour to the rescue, not on a white charger but figuratively on a model locomotive. He was W.J. Bassett-Lowke, a name I have known since my childhood, not as a rescuer of derelict railways but as the person or persons (I thought there might be a Mr Bassett and a Mr Lowke) who along with Mr Hornby invented the

Above: 'River Mite' *built 1966 by H. Clarkson & Son, York for the R. & E.R. Preservation Society.*

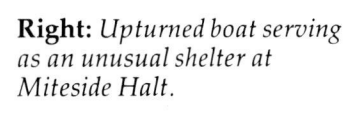

Right: *Upturned boat serving as an unusual shelter at Miteside Halt.*

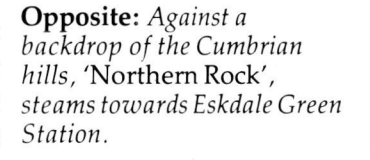

Opposite: *Against a backdrop of the Cumbrian hills, 'Northern Rock', steams towards Eskdale Green Station.*

toy train. But in Eskdale Bassett-Lowke is still remembered and revered as the man who brought 't' la'l Ratty' to life again.

He decided it was an ideal place to test his scale-model locos, and he rebuilt it with 15-inch track – except for the final gradient to Boot, which was too steep for his little engines. Instead he rebuilt the little branch line to its present terminus at Dalegarth.

It was the beginning of a new era. What started as a testbed for model engines developed into a regular train service carrying passengers, goods, and the Royal Mail. Another gallant knight – this time a real one, Sir Aubrey Brocklebank – opened a quarry at Beckfoot and provided more freight for the railway, so much in fact that in 1925 he took the railway over, and it stayed in his family until 1949. Then it was sold to a granite company, but at a time unfortunately of extreme competition in the industry, and the railway's roller-coaster existence started heading downwards again. The local quarry lost trade to rivals in more accessible areas and was closed down in 1953. Again the railway struggled on for a few years, but again it failed to make ends meet. It was placed on the market, nobody made an acceptable offer, and in 1960 it was put up for auction.

Enter Douglas Ferreira and Graham Withers. Douglas had spent holidays in the area for most of his life – 'I was first photographed beside one of the engines at the age of about three'. He served in the Merchant Navy, then got a job selling Bond mini-cars when he heard about the auction. He also heard that a preservation society was being formed, and he became involved himself. As the outside representative for his car firm he was able to travel the country, liaising with other enthusiasts and helping to raise money. He was in the village hall at Gosforth on September 7th, 1960, when the preservation society made the successful bid of £14,000.

Douglas told me laconically what happened next. 'After the railway had been saved they were looking for someone to run it, and I was looking for a job. I've been doing it ever since.'

Inside the locomotive cab of 'Northern Rock' probably the most powerful 15'' gauge engine in the world.

Opposite: 'River Mite' *steams around the rugged promontory at Rock Point.*

It was a formidable task. The line was virtually derelict, the winter months lay ahead, there were staff to be paid, work to be done on the rolling stock and engines. But under his management the railway started running again, and the improvements have continued ever since. He has just finished re-laying the entire line with new rails and sleepers – 'That will be someone else's headache in eighty or a hundred years' time!' – there are new workshops and sheds, new station buildings, new coaching stock, and new engines, the latest of which they have built themselves. There are now six steam locos and six diesels, with five fulltime staff to drive them. They do not, incidentally, include Douglas Ferreira: 'I like watching them and I know a good deal about them, but I have no desire to drive them. I only do it in an emergency.'

Not so, Graham Withers, who was once the regular driver of one of the steam locomotives, *River Mite*. Graham is substantially built, and *River Mite*, while not exactly a mite, is none too roomy. 'I was measured for the tender, just like you're measured for a suit!' That was in the early days, when he joined the railway full-time after working as a volunteer.

'Douglas offered me the job in 1964. At that time I was working as a signalman with BR. Panel signal-boxes were just coming in, and jobs were going on seniority. I worked out that it would be about 31 years before I got into a panel-box, so I took the job.'

In those days there was no signal box at Ravenglass, no console, no radio links. Trains just ran to a timetable which was planned so that they met at the loop at Irton Road; the rest of the line was all single-track. At busy times the trains were run in two or three sections, and the first engine carried a white disc to warn the oncoming driver to wait on the loop until the ones behind had gone through. It sounds a little primitive compared with the present electronic system, but there were no problems and I suspect that in Graham's opinion it worked just as well. But as the operation built up, two more passing places were added, so the line now has four sections, and an electronic 'ticket' was introduced for entering each single track.

In due course this was developed into the present system, the 'absolute block', which involves not only electronic signals but graphs and instruction sheets and radio links with all the drivers. Graham was appointed Controller and put in charge. He told me how the imposing console in front of him was an example of the enterprise shown by the railway's volunteer supporters. One of them is a German lecturer who instructed his students how to make the parts. 'He got them drilling holes in pieces of metal, not knowing what they were for, then he brought the pieces over and made them up into this console.'

He paused to take a phone call from one of the volunteer workers who man the stations and act as guards on the trains. Drawing up their rotas is another of the Controller's little chores, and as they come from all over the country to work for odd weeks or weekends, this is no mean task. Then he turned back to the console.

'The disadvantage of this system is that someone has to be here all the time; I've worked it out that I send four hundred radio messages every day. But the advantage is that if there's an emergency on the line, a fell fire for example, we can do something about it straight away.'

Sometimes the fell fires are started by sparks from the engines, though cigarette ends can be to blame too. Even in a wet summer the wind soon dries out the bracken, and a fire can soon take hold. I suppose for a steam enthusiast, it is about the only good thing to be said for a diesel.

The diesel drivers would not agree. I met one or two of them, dressed in slacks and shirts and even ties, compared with the overalls and black shiny caps of the steam men, and they were just as happy with their engines, though in a very different way. Every steam driver I have ever met can wax enthusiastic about the charms and foibles of an engine, the intricacies of its steam pressures and water levels, how it likes to have its fire laid, the best way to handle it on a gradient. They can be finicky about the coal it uses – apparently the quality can vary, even from the same seam.

Then I asked one of the shirt-sleeved young men what it was like to drive a diesel and he said simply: 'Dead easy. There's just the brake and the throttle. Keep your eye open to see you don't run over anything, and that's it...'

Douglas Ferreira reckons that a lot of young people prefer the diesels to the steam engines. In their view presumably, the little locos arouse no sentimental nostalgia, they just seem an anachronism. But I couldn't check with any young people on the train I travelled on, because there didn't seem to be any – just middle-aged and elderly folk, and couples with very small children. It was a steam train, so maybe that proves the point.

Interesting, these passengers on the Ravenglass & Eskdale. Few of them were staying locally, probably because there aren't many places to stay anyway, and judging by the hotel I was in, they were full of energetic, earnest people in long socks and large boots, who came to climb the fells under their own steam –

Waiting for the Ravenglass train at Irton Road Station.

Opposite: 'Northern Rock' *pulling into Muncaster Mill.*

33

or perhaps that should be up-dated: under their own diesel. The people on the train had mostly come from other Lakeland resorts, just for the ride up the valley, and were not too bothered about what they found at the top; a lot of them just came straight down again. The fellwalkers and the traingoers seem to form separate communities in Eskdale, but they share one enjoyment – the marvellous views.

I got the chance to enjoy them from the footplate of *River Esk*, a 1923 engine lovingly maintained, washed, polished and driven by a former schoolmaster, Peter van Zeller. We had first met outside the engine sheds, where Peter was washing down the tender with a cotton rag. A cotton rag, incidentally, is a vital piece of equipment in engine sheds, and the Ravenglass & Eskdale gets through vast quantities of old cotton shirts and sheets and underwear, all kindly donated by wellwishers and much appreciated by Peter and his colleagues.

He stood back to admire the gleaming engine. 'Effectively,' he said, 'I am being paid for what a lot of people would do for nothing. But don't tell the manager I said so.'

'What happens if it breaks down?' I asked innocently. Peter looked slightly shocked. Breaking down,

I gathered, is not the sort of thing that steam engines do. It's diesels that break down.

'A diesel has three times the power of a steam engine, but if it stops, it stops, and that's it. A steam engine is basically a very simple machine. There's just a certain number of elements involved – the draught through the fire, the coal you put on... You just have to work out what that nasty noise is, or why has that noise stopped when it ought to be going on. You can generally do something about it, and the passengers probably won't ever know. If something happens up the line it's up to me to make the judgment: can we keep going, or has it really...' and he said the words distastefully – '...broken down.'

He forgave me for my indiscretion, and now we were in the cab of *River Esk*, embarking on what the Ravenglass & Eskdale brochure describes unequivocally as The Most Beautiful Train Journey in England. You might not think so at first. Ravenglass itself is pleasant enough, once a Roman stronghold, then a medieval port until the channel silted up, then a market town until the coastal railway took the trade away, and now a pleasant village down a quiet dead end, with only the Ravenglass & Eskdale to attract the attention of tourists. But once we emerged from the houses on to the mudflats of Barrow Marsh the landscape was dominated by the massive structures a few miles up the coast, the cooling towers of Sellafield nuclear power station.

There must be a curious love-hate relationship with Sellafield among the locals. It is employment to some, anathema to others. The tourist literature for the area seems to ignore its existence, fearing perhaps it would deter the tourists, and yet it is actually a tourist attraction. Since its visitors' centre was opened in 1988 – invitingly described as 'a window on the nuclear world' – it has had some forty thousand visitors a

Left: *Eskdale Green village and the Outward Bound Mountain School are served by Green Station.*

Right: *'Northern Rock' coasting down Holling How Bank into Eskdale Green.*

year, two thousand on one Easter Monday alone. There is a walk inside a mock-up reactor, a coach ride around the power station, and a visit to the new complex called THORP, which in Norfolk is a traditional name for a village but at Sellafield means something a little less homely, Thermal Oxide Reprocessing Plant.

The whole object, of course, is to stress how jolly safe it all is. Not everybody is convinced, but I was reassured on one point when I went to Sellafield myself, as a follow-up to the ride on the Ravenglass & Eskdale. Outside the plant I saw literally hundreds of deserted cars parked along the roadside, and at 9.30 on a Sunday morning this was a little disquieting. Could they belong to previous visitors who had been absorbed into this terrifying place, never to emerge again?

No, said the official guide when I asked her, they belonged to building workers who had to board a bus to enter the site, and the bus stop was all of a hundred yards from the official car park, so they left their cars on the grass verge instead. It was quite illegal and they sometimes got parking tickets, but the British working man, it seems, prefers risking a parking ticket to walking a hundred yards. I should have been shocked but I was actually quite relieved: I looked like getting out safely after all...

Sellafield is a very different world from the Ravenglass & Eskdale, and we were able to forget it once *River Esk* left the flat landscape behind and arrived at Muncaster Mill, where power has been generated for over five hundred years, not by nuclear fission but just water and gravity. It is the only tourist attraction which the railway publicises all along the track – which is not surprising, because the railway owns it. The derelict building was bought in 1975 to be converted into staff accommodation, but it turned out to be less derelict than they thought, and a couple of years later the great waterwheel was turning again to produce stone-ground flour. It was the conservationist answer to Megawatt Mansion just along the coast...

Into the woods now and up the valley alongside Muncaster Fell, with the conical peak of Scafell straight ahead. At a steady 14 miles an hour we passed the curious passenger shelter at Miteside Halt. A thirty-foot boat has been cut through the middle, and one half of it turned on end and planted beside the track; five or six people can just about stand inside it. If it ever falls down or rots away, no doubt they have still got the other half somewhere to replace it.

The remains of Murthwaite crushing plant still stand rather bleakly beside the line. This was where they ground the granite from Beckfoot Quarry, further up the valley. It was one of the hardest stones in the country, much in demand for construction work; the concrete in London's Waterloo Bridge originated from this remote little crushing plant hidden in the trees at the foot of Muncaster Fell.

Peter van Zeller slowed *River Esk* as we emerged from the woods on to a fairly narrow ledge around a promontory, with only two or three feet clearance between the train and a long drop down to the River Mite. 'This is Rock Point. When they built the original

Opposite: 'River Irt' *climbing through Gilbert's Cutting.*

'Northern Rock' *on the turntable at Dalegarth.*

three-foot gauge it was right on the edge of a sheer drop – it must have been a bit more exciting in those days. Then the Ministry inspector insisted the ledge should be widened – but it's still quite interesting.'

I was on the side nearest the drop, and yes, it was still quite interesting...

Irton Road is the line's only original station, and it still has the stone-built shelter and booking-office. Confusingly, it is nowhere near Irton village, famous for the ninth-century Celtic Cross which was erected in the churchyard at a time when Muncaster Mill would have seemed the height of modern technology. The station actually serves one end of Eskdale Green village, while the Green station serves the other. The village hardly seems to rate one station, let alone two, but in the world of little trains, population figures don't count.

We climbed steadily up the valley, on its northern flank now, with steep bracken-covered hillside above us and rich farmland below, with the River Esk just visible beyond. Then we entered something of a rarity

'Northern Rock' taking on water at Fisherground Loop, the third passing place on the line.

for Little Ratty, a cutting. Peter explained how it came about.

'Until 1963 the line made a series of sharp curves around Holling Head bend. One of my first memories of the line was the squealing of the wheels on those curves. It didn't do the engines any good at all – or the track. So they built this cutting through the bluff to make the curve gentler. They had to shift three thousand tons of rock and lay seven hundred feet of new track – quite an effort.'

Actually it was a most remarkable effort, probably the biggest earth-moving exercise ever carried out on a 15-inch gauge railway. No wonder the penny-pinching Ratcliff took the easy route.

We had a glimpse of the old Beckfoot Quarry, once the scene of an even more spectacular earth-moving feat. When it was closed, it went out with a bang; for the final firing they used four tons of explosives and dislodged more than sixty thousand tons of granite, the biggest explosion in its history, But nobody has pressed a plunger at Beckfoot since 1953. A couple of the old quarry buildings still stand, but the miners have moved out of the cottages alongside the line and railway staff have moved in.

Peter brought *River Esk* into Dalegarth Station, the end of the line. We were in the heart of the fells now, with Scafell and Harter Fell on the skyline to right and left of us, and Crinkle Crags in between. If any of my fellow hotel guests had been on board they would have headed off now to Wastwater or Hardknott Pass or the Esk Falls, all within range for what the guide-book calls 'an enthusiastic walker'. The less enthusiastic, which seemed to cover most of us, headed for the station snack-bar or watched Peter turn *River Esk*, pushing it round by hand on the little turntable. Impressive to see an engine which had hauled a train-load seven miles up the valley, now pushed round single-handed by its driver – but that's what little trains are all about.

Well, not *all* about. Little Ratty is not just a grown-up version of playing trains with steam engines, they actually build the engines as well. This little company

has managed to reverse an international trend. We are used to the Japanese copying British products and selling them back to us, but in the Ravenglass workshops they are copying their own products and selling them to the Japanese.

It is a miniature version of what used to be a major export business, in the days when Britain supplied Japan with main-line steam locomotives. The Japanese built a leisure park outside Tokyo, featuring a half-timbered Tudor-style English village, and wanted a 15-inch gauge railway to go with it. The Tudors and 15-inch railways were not exactly contemporary, but perhaps the Japanese are not too strong on English industrial history, and in a leisure park, who cares

anyway? They came over to the country which used to supply the full-sized models, and gravitated to Ravenglass, where they had just built their own latest engine, *Northern Rock*.

The visitors saw *Northern Rock* and promptly ordered an exact replica. *Northern Rock II* was shipped to Japan early in 1990 and proved so successful that a year later they ordered another one. So England's oldest narrow-gauge railway has entered England's newest export business, at present just to Japan, but why stop there? It could be the launchpad for pastures and leisure parks new.

As they might well say on the Ravenglass & Eskdale: 'Ratty...saki...Go!'

'River Irt' steams down towards Irton Road Station.

Wells & Walsingham Light Railway

I HAVE to confess, Norfolk is my favourite county. We can't boast the wild remoteness of the Yorkshire moors, because the Norfolk soil is too rich to be left to the hikers and the heather. We don't have the picture-postcard timber and thatch of the West Country, because our cottages are built of flint-stone and pantiles to stand up to the Norfolk winter. And although our countryside is not nearly as feature-less as Noel Coward made out – remember his 'Very flat, Norfolk?' – it hardly matches the formidable contours of the Cumbrian fells. To the casual visitor, it may merely look like one damn' field after another...

But there are some delightful discoveries to be made down these apparently unpromising lanes. There are great mansions and tiny village greens, peaceful woods and secluded streams, quaint little pubs and magnificent medieval churches – and not least, there is the Wells & Walsingham Light Railway.

You may have heard of Wells, once a notable port until the sea withdrew across the salt marshes, leaving a channel only deep enough for small coastal shipping and the local whelkboats – and Wells became Wells-next-the-Sea. It is more likely you will have heard of Walsingham, where the Lady of the Manor had a vision of the Virgin Mary, back in the days of Edward the Confessor, and it has been a centre for pilgrimage ever since. But far fewer people know about the little railway line that connects Walsingham and Wells, even though it has a remarkable place in the record books. It is the world's longest 10¼-inch gauge railway; it is also the smallest public railway in the world.

Its tiny track, invisible from the road for much of its

'Norfolk Hero', *pulling a Walsingham-bound train.*

41

Wells & Walsingham Railway

Wells-next-to-the-Sea, Norfolk, NR23 1QB.
No telephone

Route: Wells – Walsingham
Distance: 4 miles
Gauge: 10¼ in
Service: Daily, Good Friday – end Sept.

This little line, opened in 1982, uses trackbed previously built by the Wells & Fakenham Railway for its standard gauge line between the towns, opened on 1 December 1857. There must however be a very good chance that the route now sees a great deal more traffic that it ever did in its standard gauge days – it was due to a shortage of this very necessary commodity that the 'big' line closed in 1964, after which it was dismantled and the land sold off. It was some little time before work began on the new project, but things were put in hand in 1979, and a service eventually began using *Pilgrim*, a small 0-4-0 steam locomotive and a minimum number of carriages. Four of the original nine miles of trackbed were utilised, running inland to a point just short of the old Walsingham station, a journey involving a climb of 1 in 29. This was not the gradient of the original railway, but was now necessary to surmount infill in one of the cuttings. The new railway was a great success – so much so that it was soon found that extra carriages and a more powerful engine were desperately needed. This problem has now been solved by the largest 10¼-inch gauge locomotive ever built, a Beyer-Garratt type double engine, which has been christened *Norfolk Hero*.

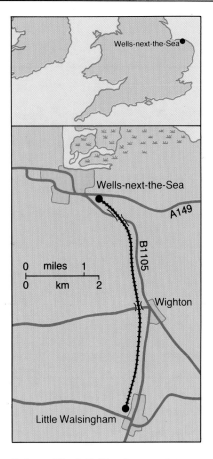

Below: 'Norfolk Hero' *name plate.*

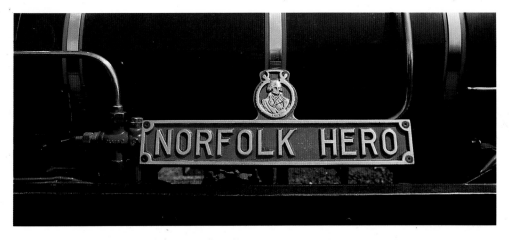

route, threads its way through the rolling, empty countryside of what would logically be called Deep Norfolk, but in these parts – because they like to 'du diff'rent' – they call it High Norfolk. If you were not told where to look for it, you would probably never know it was there.

It was not ever thus. When I first lived in Norfolk in the nineteen-fifties, there was a network of branch lines throughout the county, linking Norwich with Dereham and King's Lynn, and King's Lynn with Wells and Cromer, and back from Cromer to Norwich. The line I travelled on regularly was the old Great Eastern from Dereham to Wells, and the steam trains took me alongside the River Wensum to Fakenham, and then on northwards to the four W's – Walsingham, Wighton, Warham and Wells. When the steam trains were withdrawn we thought the line would go too, but the diesel railcars came instead to bring a brief reprieve. I travelled on the first railcar, hoping to take part in a celebration, but throughout the journey there were only four people on board – the driver, the guard, a young trainspotter, and me. It takes more than one schoolboy and a local reporter to keep a line going, and with all the other Norfolk branch lines it was lopped off by the Beeching Axe, leaving just the two main lines from London, to Norwich and Great Yarmouth in the east and to King's Lynn in the west. On the map they form a 'V', like two mocking fingers...

The stations between Dereham and Fakenham were dismantled or converted, part of the trackbed became a nature trail. Walsingham station was turned into a place of worship, and for many years the trackbed between Walsingham and Wells was left derelict. One section of it, passing through a deep cutting, was used by the local council to dump rubbish. It seemed impossible that either Walsingham or Wells-next-the-Sea would ever have a train service again. But fifteen years after the diesel railcars made their last run and the line was taken up, the first length of new track was

Right: 'Norfolk Hero' *climbing hard through Barnard Cutting.*

re-laid, not standard gauge but the much tinier 10¼-inch. And three years after that, in March 1982, the trains started running regularly again on what was now the Wells & Walsingham Light Railway.

It was due entirely to one remarkable man, who dreamed up the idea of the railway, financed it, launched it, and still personally operates it. His name is Lieutenant-Commander Roy Francis R.N. (Retd).

Britain is rich in train enthusiasts, but few would be enthusiastic enough to mortgage their homes in order to build a railway, at a time of life when most people are trying to plan a secure retirement. Roy Francis did just that, and so fulfilled an ambition he had cherished since he visited the Romney, Hythe & Dymchurch as a small boy.

'I'm going to be an engine driver,' he told his father.

'Um,' said his father, or words to that effect, and put him on board a Royal Naval training ship instead. For the next twenty-five years or so, Roy had to forget about trains and concentrate on ships. He also had to concentrate on survival – particularly on the North Russian convoys. He was serving on board *HMS Edinburgh* when it was sunk on the way home. He was rescued from the Arctic waters and taken back to Murmansk, where he spent some weeks waiting for a ship. 'It was a terrible place to be. The Germans were only fifteen miles away, and we all expected the Russians would say, 'Right, here's a rifle – off you go!'

Many years later the Russians gave him, not a rifle, but a medal. He had to go to their Embassy in London to get it, and when his train arrived late at Liverpool Street – as trains are rather wont to do – he took great delight in giving the taxi-driver the classic command: 'Take me to the Russian Embassy – as fast as you can!'

After the war he commanded salvage ships clearing harbours of sunken wreckage, from West Africa to Hong Kong, and during the East coast gales of 1953 he rescued the Scottish herring fleet when it was blown ashore. He came to know a lot about small boats as well as large ones, and when he left the Navy in 1958 it seemed logical to stay with them, so he acquired a boat yard on the Norfolk Broads and a fleet of cabin cruisers. But while he knew plenty about boats, he knew rather less about business. The venture proved a disaster.

In his spare time, however, he was already back into steam trains. He managed to buy a circular 7½-inch gauge track for £12, just the right length to go round his house, plus a few carriages and an engine he partially built himself. When the boatyard business got shaky he tried taking his railway to a country fair, and took £35 – more in a day than he could afford to pay himself at the boatyard in a week. So the retired naval officer sold up and started a new career as a travelling showman, touring the country in a lorry with a 29-foot trailer, and operating his little train at agricultural shows and carnivals and anywhere else that would have him.

It was an exhausting business, unloading and assembling the track, running the train all day, then loading up the lorry and trailer and driving overnight from perhaps a County Show in Shropshire to a

Left: *The 10¼'' track was laid on the old B.R. trackbed.*

Right: *'Norfolk Hero' taking on water at Wells Station.*

carnival in Braintree. Then another day of unloading and assembling, and driving, and dismantling and loading...

At last relief came. 'I was running the train on a car park at East Runton, near Cromer, at a time when there were no shows to visit, and North Norfolk Council invited me to lay and operate a permanent line from Wells town down to the beach – that's just over half-a-mile. It came at just the right time; I was really beginning to get too old for all this driving around and humping about.'

He laid the 10¼-inch line and it was an immediate success. The distance is just too far for some holiday-makers to walk, but not worth getting out the car. And for Roy Francis himself it was a taste of bigger and better things to come. He had got his eye on the old British Railways line to Walsingham, and when he walked the four miles along the trackbed he found that, apart from the rubbish-filled cutting, it was still in reasonable shape. So were the five bridges along the route. The line would have to stop short outside Wells because there was no longer a crossing over the main coast road, and at Walsingham too the original station was no longer accessible, but there was still a clear run – apart from that cutting – in between. He decided to go ahead.

I have to say that Roy Francis is not the popular image of a retired Naval officer; he is a soft-spoken, almost self-effacing man. But when it comes to Little Trains, he has enormous determination and perseverance. He mortgaged his house to pay for the line, and when that proved insufficient he sold the beach railway. Inevitably his original estimate of what it would cost had to be doubled – and then there was that blocked-up cutting...

But help began to pour in. In particular there was Gary Jay, who joined him in the early days and still manages the business side of the railway for him, as well as taking his turn at driving, maintaining the track, putting up the odd building... 'He's my right-hand-man'. And there is the only other fulltime worker on the Wells & Walsingham, Steve Tuck, born

Lt. Cmdr. Roy Francis giving 'Norfolk Hero' *a final polish.*

Inside the cab of 'Norfolk Hero', *a Garratt type locomotive designed by Neil Simkins.*

Right: *The last train of the day.*

and bred in Wells, one of the first volunteers laying the track and now the regular guard.

Other volunteers joined in too, clearing the trackbed, spreading fresh ballast, laying new track. 'A 15-inch gauge would probably have been more profitable,' Roy Francis admits, 'because it could have taken more passengers. But it would have been just another 15-inch railway, and not a very long one at that. I wanted the Wells and Walsingham to be different from all the others.'

So down it went, eighteen-foot lengths of 10¼-inch track, twelve hundred lengths. But then there was that cutting...

This was where Ken Barnard came in. Ken provided a digger-loader and two tipper lorries, complete with drivers. Four days after the Council had dumped its last load of refuse, Ken Barnard's men, with Roy Francis and his volunteers, started clearing it out again. The original gradient through the cutting was 1-in-40, but after taking out three thousand tons of rubbish it was decided to leave it at 1-in-29 – one of the steepest railway gradients in the country. When the time came to settle Ken's bill, he refused to take the money. But his generosity is not forgotten; a sign beside the track proclaims that this is *Barnard Cutting.*

While all this was going on, Roy Francis cleared another vital hurdle. He obtained a Light Railway Order from the Department of Transport, entitling him to run a regular public passenger service. In March 1982 the first train left Wells for Walsingham. It has been running throughout the summer months, seven days a week, six times each way at peak times, ever since.

The Wells terminus was fairly basic in the early days, and it hasn't changed much since. It is one of Roy Francis's great regrets that nearly all the railway buildings along that stretch of line have disappeared, and all that is left at the Wells end of the line is a signal-box. On the far side of the main road, where the line used to continue into the town, there is the crossing-keeper's house, now inaccessible from the Wells & Walsingham. It was the home for many years

of Joe the crossing-keeper, and it is still called, agonisingly, *Josabode*...

The terminus does now boast a rather battered engine-shed and an even more battered old caravan, where Roy Francis camps out throughout the summer. It also seems to be a sort of communal restroom for his helpers, and the wear and tear is beginning to show, but when I last saw Roy he was planning to convert the top floor of the signal-box into a one-room flat, and he may be ensconced there by now, above the booking-office and shop. At the Walsingham end there is even less, just a platform where passengers wait for the train. They have nothing to shelter under, but most of the train carriages have no roofs either, so it is a useful acclimatisation exercise...

The biggest change in the past ten years has been the engine. Roy started out with *Pilgrim*, built specially for the line by a Norfolk company. It was a doggy little engine with two big round windows in the cab, a fairly small boiler and a very tall funnel – straight out of a child's picture-book. It could haul five coaches and about fifty passengers, but no more – that 1-in-29 gradient through Barnard Cutting would have been too much for it. Roy acquired a petrol engine in 1985 which could haul bigger loads and was used as a standby, but he knew that a steam engine was the real attraction and he tried to use it only for maintenance work. The search began for a steam replacement for *Pilgrim,* powerful enough to haul twice the load up Barnard Cutting, but small enough to run on a 10¼-inch railway. It also had to be reliable enough to run continuously throughout the season; that meant a total of six thousand miles.

Enter Neil Simkins, consulting engineer...

Mr Simkins came and inspected the line, discovered how it was operated – and reacted with a mixture of admiration and disbelief. 'To the traditional railway-man,' he wrote later, 'this high mileage, tight turn-round, long unbroken service period with no spare equipment and only the simplest of hand tools,

Left: *Walsingham-bound train passing through wheat fields.*

sounds like a recipe for exasperation, failure and disaster. Not so our gallant Commander, whose philosophy to the operation of machinery is to ask, 'Why don't ships have spare engines, then?'

He was not too impressed with the rolling-stock either, 'It provides a level of comfort, exposure to weather, speed and frequency of service remarkably similar to that offered by the very early railways.' As for the track, the most flattering word he could think of was 'indifferent'. Finally, he summed up the Wells & Walsingham in a way which has now become something of a catchword among those who work on it: 'The Wibbly-Wobbly Railway.'

Nevertheless, Neil Simkins undertook to design a Garratt engine which would do the job that Roy Francis wanted. In 1986 he produced the largest and most powerful 10¼-inch gauge locomotive ever constructed, and the first one to go into service on a public railway in Britain for nearly half-a-century. It was named, like so many pubs in this part of Norfolk close to Nelson's birthplace, *Norfolk Hero*.

There is a complicated technical description of *Norfolk Hero,* involving boiler cradle pivot centres and buffalo injections to top feed valves, but basically it is three separate sections linked together, the cab and boiler in the middle, and water tanks fore and aft – 78 gallons in front, 68 at the rear – so the load is spread over a long wheelspan and the centre of gravity is kept low. Even so, like the carriages it is considerably wider than the rails, and it seems astonishing at first glance that the whole train doesn't tip over – particularly if a hundred passengers all decide to get off simultaneously on the same side.

The answer, as I should have known as an ex-broadcaster, is articulation. Not in this case clarity of speech, but overlapping the sections of engine and all the carriages so that no individual chassis can tilt without all the others. Even if it did, the train is so close to the ground that the edge would touch before it could tip right over. In fact, Roy assured me that it could all be two or three inches wider with perfect safety.

We could have done with those extra inches when

he invited me to join him in the cab of *Norfolk Hero*. I looked at the size of us, and the size of the cab, and hesitated. Then I noticed that I was getting envious looks from all the passengers behind us, and I hesitated no longer. We wedged ourselves into the tiny seat, our knees intimately pressed together to avoid the hot metal a few inches in front of us, Roy sounded the whistle – surely the most rewarding part of driving a steam engine – and we were away.

The rolling farmland of High Norfolk is very familiar to me, but one gets quite a different view of it from a seat in a small steam train, just a few inches above the rails. The first bridge we went under, known rather grandly as *The Tunnel*, because it is built at an angle and thus longer than most, seemed as lofty as a cathedral. Then we were in a cutting where the banks towered above us on both sides, riddled with rabbit-holes. If the rabbits had wanted to stage an ambush they could easily have leapt down into our laps.

Out into the open again on a high embankment, and an elevated view of the fields stretching away for miles on either side. On a distant hillside there was the circular mound of Warham's Iron Age fort, but all we saw of latter-day Warham was a crossing keeper's cottage, lonely and deserted alongside the line, its *For Sale* notice almost as old, it seemed, as the cottage itself. But what a find for a reclusive railway buff, I thought. Nobody else for miles, just *Norfolk Hero* puffing past the garden twelve times a day during the summer, available for a gentle ride into town on request...

Wighton village lies away from the line as well, but it is clearly visible across the fields, a cluster of flint cottages around the parish church, and I remembered the fairytale story of the church tower. It was blown down in a gale in 1965, and lay in ruins for years until a rich Canadian happened to visit the village to trace his ancestors. He saw the ruined tower, and gave a hundred thousand dollars to rebuild it, which was enough for a new peal of bells as well. They named it the Trillium Tower in his honour, after the national

'Norfolk Hero' *on the level crossing of the old Wighton Station.*

flower of Ontario, as well they might. Neighbouring parishes hoping for a grant from English Heritage to save their churches must be pondering, not 'Why are we waiting?' but 'Why aren't we Wighton...'

The village used to have a station, but only the overgrown platform is left. It loomed alongside us at head level, a reminder of just how low we were sitting. And compared with the size of the platform, the track ahead looked more like a toy than ever, as it stretched away in a straight line – well, a fairly straight line – into the once-noisome Barnard Cutting. A certain aroma lingers in this area if the wind is right, not from the cutting but from Walsingham Sewage Works alongside the track, a forceful indication that a sizable community lies ahead.

The first houses to come into sight are in Great Walsingham, so named in 'du diff'rent' Norfolk because it is much smaller than Little Walsingham. It is also a lot quieter, because all the pilgrims and tourists head for the shrines and curio shops of Little Walsingham. That is where the train goes too, through the backyards of a housing estate where geese and

Opposite: *Side view of the 1986-built Garratt.*

Return journey of 'Norfolk Hero' *through Barnard Cutting.*

Wells & Walsingham; he has been on nearly every train for the last five years, collecting the fares, chatting up the passengers, dealing with obstreperous children, and generally keeping the wheels turning in his own way, just as the driver does in *Norfolk Hero.*

In his gentle Norfolk accent he told me how he returned to Wells on holiday, years after he had helped to lay the track, and travelled on the train to visit a friend. 'Roy jump on beside me and he say, "How'd you like to do guard, then?" And I say to him, 'Yes, I'd love to'. And I did it for two or three weeks, then he ask me to do it permanent, like.' He beamed at me. 'Thass a nice job – it's grand doing a job you enjoy. But you do get a little tired going up and down, up and down, all the day long...'

Looking around, I could understand how he felt. I hadn't done the trip twice yet, but the scenery was becoming quite familiar, even from this angle. Steve looked around too.

'I know every inch of this line now. I'd know it with my eyes shut – I recognise the bumps! Or if I'm reading a book for a bit I can cock my eyes up and see a piece of bank, and know exactly where I am. But that do change during the season – different flowers to look at for a start. And there's all the rabbits, o'course. They have the rabbit control during the winter, game-keepers shooting them by the hundred, but they can't get on top of 'em – you won't stop 'em now.'

I remembered the cutting with all the rabbit holes. Maybe an ambush wasn't impossible after all...

I changed the subject. 'Do you have any trouble with the passengers? Children larking about, perhaps?'

Steve nodded sagely. 'That don't happen often, but when it does, then you have to be diplomatic and just tell then very nicely to stop, and they mostly do. But very often I get told off then by the parents...'

I looked along the 'toastrack' carriages. Manifestly the Wells & Walsingham did not go in for corridors. 'How about if you're one end of the train and there's trouble at the other?'

'Well then, you have to gestickerlate at 'em,' said

hens gazed at us unconcernedly as we trundled past, their eyes on a level with ours.

The line peters out as we reached the road, and our arrival might have been something of an anti-climax except for the holidaymakers waiting with their cameras to give us the star treatment. For Roy Francis this is a familiar routine, but for me, waving graciously out of my side of the cab, it was a rare taste of glory. It must be quite gratifying for the other drivers too – the retired doctor, the former bank manager, the agricultural engineer, and the other volunteers who occupy the cab of *Norfolk Hero.*

But while the driver changes, the guard remains the same, and I travelled back to Wells in his company. You can tell that Steve Tuck is the guard because he wears a waistcoat and jacket and sits in the compartment marked *Guard,* but you might not guess otherwise. He still sports the long straight hair and short straight beard which was all the rage among the 'flower people' in the Sixties, and British Rail might not entirely approve. But Steve is a key figure on the

Steve patiently. 'And if that don't work, then you have to drop the anchors and stop the train, and have a little word. If you do it nicely, you don't get any trouble.'

I persevered. 'Any drunks?'

Steve chuckled. 'I've had a few from Walsingham during the pilgrimages. I expect they need a bit of relaxation after all that walking. They're just pleasantly oiled, I'd say. They mostly doze off on the seats; they're no problem.'

I began to fancy 'doing guard' myself – it seemed quite a halcyon existence. But Steve had a second thought. 'Mind you, I do meet some rum characters. There was this lady got on the train, and she asked if there were any concessions for OAPs. Well, she looked too young to be an OAP, sincerely she did, so I say as a bit of a compliment, like: 'You don't look old enough to be an OAP'. And do you know, she come at me and she say, 'You rotten little sod', she say, and she got out the carriage and hit me three times over the head with her umbrella!'

He felt his head ruefully at the memory. 'I was sort o' stunned, you know, but the rest of the staff, they were in stitches, hanging onto the side of the signal-box laughing, they were, and the passengers were pretending not to laugh but they were, o' course. To this day I can't understand what she thought I said. She must've heard something really nasty, but all I was doing was trying to be nice, and then – lump, lump, lump over the head...'

The story had sparked off more memories. 'Then there's the people who argue about how much the fare costs, though that's cheap if you think what it cost to run this railway. I tell 'em, 'This hent public transport, you know, you're out for a joy-ride' – and then they think you're being offensive, like.' He looked gloomy for a moment, but he soon cheered up 'That don't happen often, though. The nice people outweigh the awk'd ones, thass for sure. It's a really nice job, this.' Even so, I decided maybe I wouldn't 'do guard' after all.

We were coming to the terminus at Wells and a white-haired figure in stained blue overalls and the statutory shiny black cap was waiting by the line to change the points. As *Norfolk Hero* passed him he exchanged a wave with Roy Francis in the cab, and we waved to each other too. 'He's a university professor,' said Steve casually. 'He often comes to help out – he's a really nice man.'

The train came to a stop, and as we got out, the guard of the Wells & Walsingham Light Railway gave me another beam through the beard and the long straight hair. 'But then,' he said, 'they're all nice people that come to work on this railway. That's the sort of railway it is...'

There are plans, of course, for making the Wells & Walsingham a little more sophisticated. More closed carriages, perhaps, a proper station building at each terminus, toilets, a buffet. There is already a smart new repair shed up the line. But I prefer to picture Lt.-Cdr. Roy Francis R.N. (Retd) sitting in that dilapidated caravan by the end of the line, a relic of his old pioneering days, watching the holidaymakers piling into those open wooden seats behind *Norfolk Hero*, and seeing a dream come true.

Shunting of 'Norfolk Hero' into its loco shed at Wells Station.

Snowdon Mountain Railway

THE voice over the loudspeaker in the station forecourt had the proper blend of urgency and bonhomie, with a faint Welsh lilt to it.

'The booking office is now open for the sale of tickets on the next train to the Summit. The train will be leaving at 10.30. Get your tickets now, please...'

A final 'Roll up, roll up!' would not have been out of place, because there is a distinct fairground flavour about the Snowdon Mountain Railway. It could be a giant-size version of a roller-coaster, except that instead of going up and down, it goes up and up, and up, and up...

That may well have been what the Victorian creators had in mind, because they built it as a tourist attraction. It never served any useful function, like all the other narrow-gauge railways I visited. It never brought slate down from a quarry, or logs into a paper-mill, or passengers from one holiday resort to another. The Snowdon Mountain Tramroad and Hotels Company was formed in 1894 to build a steam railway which would give the public a fun-ride and the shareholders a profit, and it has been doing so, without a break, ever since.

The idea of running trains up the highest mountain in England and Wales was a splendid example of English eccentricity. It meant devoting an enormous amount of technical know-how, manual effort and hard cash to a project which in practical terms was quite pointless. Having got to the top, all they could do was turn round and come down again.

The same might be said of the first people to climb Everest, but while they climbed it 'because it was there', the railway company climbed Snowdon

A Snowdon Mountain Railway engine near the summit.

55

Snowdon Mountain Railway

Llanberis, Caernarfon, Gwynedd, LL5 4TY.
Tel. (0286) 870223

Route: Llanberis – Snowdon Summit
Distance: 4.75 miles
Gauge: 2 ft 7⁵/₈ in
Service: Daily, mid March – beginning Nov.

Not only its gauge makes this line unique in the UK, but its mode of traction, by rack and pinion, does also. Teeth on the driving axles of the locomotives engage with similar teeth in a central rail, so that the wheels of the engine actually do nothing more than carry it. The line opened in 1898, closed the same day following the only fatality the line has ever known, and re-opened in April the next year. There have been no more such setbacks, and the railway has been taking passengers to the top of Wales' highest mountain (weather permitting) ever since. For safety reasons the carriage, which has independent brakes, is always marshalled on the uphill side of the locomotive, which is not coupled to it, and whole is governed to a speed of 5mph. Entirely steam-worked until 1986, diesels were then introduced for reasons of economy. On some busy days the line can turn away as many passengers as it carries (100,000 were accommodated for the first time in a single season during 1989), but a token system now ensures that the long queues of the '50s and '60s are no more. To cope with as many as 48 train movements in one day, radio control was introduced in 1978, and this system was renewed in 1990, with the added facility that an emergency alert can be raised at the push of a button.

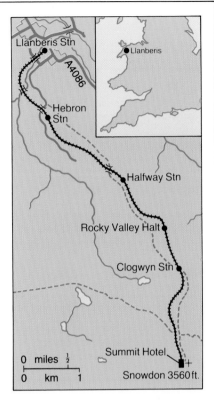

Below: *Double-track rail with out of phase teeth. On both axles of the loco are two central cog wheels which engage with the rack.*

because it was potentially a nice little earner. The hundred and fifty men who actually built it, often in the most appalling conditions, probably got the least out of it – their pay ranged from six to ten old pence a day.

While the English regarded it as a notable if rather bizarre feat of engineering, the Welsh were not quite so impressed. At that time, a hundred years ago, Snowdonia was still wild and untamed, little changed since the original Ancient Britons, the Celts, made it their stronghold against the successive onslaughts of Romans, Saxons, Danes and Normans. It was only a cunning ploy by Edward I which persuaded them to come out of the mountains and meet him at Caernarvon Castle; he told them he would create a Prince of Wales who could not speak a word of English. And when they discovered that their new prince was actually his infant son – who indeed could speak no word of English, nor any words at all – they very sensibly went back to the mountains, and re-manned the barricades.

Even when a genuine Welshman, Henry Tudor, became King of England, the Snowdonians found it difficult to refrain from thumping any Englishman that came their way, and that part of Wales has remained the heartland of Welsh culture and tradition ever since. So when the Snowdon Mountain Tramroad and Hotels Company turned up and started laying a track up to the peak which dominates Snowdonia, a peak which the Celts considered sacred, where King Arthur vanquished evil ogres, some of the locals were distinctly miffed. The Welsh term for Snowdon is 'Yr Wyddfa', and their reaction might be translated back into English as 'Ere, Waddfor?'

But the project went ahead, and two years later the first train set off up the mountain from Llanberis Station. The engine was named after the wife of the largest landowner in the area, but this could hardly have placated the Welsh, since she had the very English name of Laura Alice Duff Assheton Smith.

Right: *Steam loco climbing towards Clogwyn Station.*

The chap who had to make the nameplate was none too pleased either; how do you fit a name like that onto a very small steam engine? He took the easy way out, and just put her initials – which perhaps was quite tactful, because LADAS does sound slightly Welsh, if only to an Englishman.

It was not enough, however, to placate the Welsh gods. Something went wrong with the rack-and-pinion mechanism and the locomotive started running backwards down the mountain. The driver panicked and jumped off the footplate, killing himself in the process, and *Laura Alice Duff Assheton Smith* took a purler off the track. In the company office they still have a faded photograph of the de-railed engine, with large numbers of railwaymen gathered around, some standing, some sitting, some reclining gracefully. None of them looks particularly perturbed; maybe they were all Welsh.

It took a year to sort out the fault in the rack-and-pinion, but there have been no problems since. The device was pioneered in Switzerland and is known in the trade as the Abt system – which really would be a handy name to fit on an engine. The two rails for the wheels have a gauge of 2'7⅝", which seems a funny sort of size in feet and inches, but to the Swiss it is a logical 800 millimetres. Between these rails there is a toothed rack which engages with cogwheels on the engine axles. There are various extra safety features, but that's as far as my technical expertise goes...

A train consists of one carriage which is pushed up the mountain from behind. The engine is not actually connected to the carriage, so that if by some extraordinary mischance the engine starts running away down the mountain, LADAS-style, the brakeman in the carriage can apply the brake, and the passengers can sit there stationary, and wave the engine goodbye. It has never happened yet and is never likely to, but belts and braces are advisable on a railway which runs steeply downhill for four-and-a-half miles, sometimes on gradients of one-in-five. If an engine ever did break loose at the summit, by the time it reached the bottom it could have enough impetus to clear Llanberis Lake.

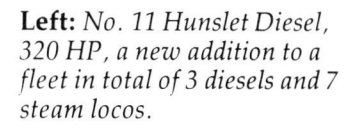

Swiss-built locomotive 'Snowdon' shunting at Llanberis Station.

Left: *No. 11 Hunslet Diesel, 320 HP, a new addition to a fleet in total of 3 diesels and 7 steam locos.*

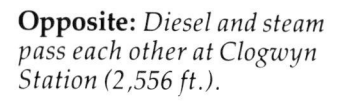

Opposite: *Diesel and steam pass each other at Clogwyn Station (2,556 ft.).*

A *Snowdon Flier* has yet to feature in the railway timetable, but if the line ever closes, what a way to dispose of surplus rolling-stock...

Normally, however, the little engines puff up and down the mountain more sedately, at a gentle five miles an hour each way. Or rather, some of them puff and others chug, because these days the seven little steam engines, all built before 1923, have been augmented by three diesels. To a steam buff, this is near sacrilege, and the drivers were not too keen at first either, but to most passengers, according to the general manager Derek Rogerson, it makes very little odds.

'Before we decided to buy diesels we were told it would be a disaster, but we found – as I rather suspected – that most people don't seem to mind what sort of engine is pushing them, because it's behind them and they can't see it anyway. We did a survey, and in marketing terms we found the attraction of the railway was 85 per cent mountain and 15 per cent steam. We do have the occasional died-in-the-wool steam buff, perhaps one a day, who gets really offended if it's not a steam train, but to be cynical about it, for every one of those who says, 'I'm not going on your so-and-so train', I've got five people waiting to take his seat. That's how we survive – we're a means of transport up the mountain, rather than a preserved steam enclave.'

Derek Rogerson is one of the few people running a narrow-gauge railway who, as you may have gathered, is not exactly a steam enthusiast himself, though he knows plenty about it. His early experience and interest as a mechanical engineer was in steam locos, and one of his first jobs was helping to get the French railways on the move again after the war. Back home again, he noted that the railways were about the poorest payers around, and in those days the mining industry was the best, so instead of taking a £5-a-week job with British Railways he took a £10-a-week job in the mines.

He started in County Durham, then worked abroad in Spain and South America, and anywhere else where mining machinery was involved. Twenty-eight years later he decided he had had enough, and in 1980 he was looking for a different career when the Snowdon Mountain Railway advertised for a general manager 'with managerial and steam experience'.

'That was a fairly rare combination. There are plenty of managers about, but not many these days with steam experience, so I got the job. It wasn't because I was very clever, it's just that the competition was very thin...' Nevertheless, he's still there.

It can't have been easy at first for the man from Cheshire to run a railway where every employee is not only a Welsh speaker but normally speaks Welsh. Although he is a good linguist and had no problems learning Spanish when he was abroad, he confesses that he found the Welsh language 'impenetrable'; the grammer seems to be quite unlike any modern European language. But Derek Rogerson is a likable, gregarious character, loquacious enough even to out-talk the Welsh, and he fared rather better in his negotiations with the locals than Edward I. One of his biggest tests was introducing his own new 'baby', the diesels.

Left: 'Padarn' *taking on water at Halfway Station (1641 ft.).*

Right: *Final push across the stony ridge of Clogwyn Coch and Cwm Glas on the approach to the summit.*

'In the local Welsh dialect I don't think they have a word which means 'change' – they're not very strong on change in Llanberis. So when we decided to introduce diesels, I had a long chat with the unions to make sure they understood why we were doing it, so we didn't have them saying they wouldn't drive them unless we gave them three million pounds an hour or something. It wasn't just converting some of them from steam to diesel. All the drivers have to be able to drive all the engines, and there are two kinds of steam so they had to learn three different techniques. At first it was like dragging teeth...'

His eyes sparkled cheerfully at the recollection – the same cheerful sparkle, I suspect, which helped to win over the drivers. 'Then I insisted they all had medicals, because diesels are OPOs, one-person operations, whereas a steam engine has a driver and fireman, and the fireman knows almost as much as the driver if there's an emergency. Though of course diesels do have a dead man's pedal, so they come to a halt automatically, whereas a steam engine only stops when you stop it, except of course when you over-steam...'

I was getting lost, and he realised it. 'Anyway, I talked with the railway inspectorate and we thought it was prudent to have medical tests, and the drivers thought there was something very sinister in that; they were sure I must be trying to get rid of some of them.'

The eyes sparkled again. 'But we got over that one, and they got used to driving the diesels, and now the ones who drive them regularly make sure that if anything goes wrong with them, it's put right in double-quick time, in case they get put back on a steam train while the diesel's out of service! Now they say to me, "We could do with more of these, Mr Rogerson" – they reckon diesels are the best thing that's ever happened.'

I was expecting the eyes to sparkle, and they did. 'You'd almost think they'd thought of it themselves, really. But they're very enthusiastic, and that's fine.'

The enthusiasm was not only because diesels are cleaner and simpler to drive. They also qualify for the top drivers' rates, and half the money saved on

Halfway Station blockman operating the passing loop for the up and down trains.

Name plate on Clogwyn Station.

Opposite: *In the heart of Snowdonia.*

running a diesel instead of a steam engine goes into the staff bonuses. These savings are quite remarkable: it costs £3.40 in diesel fuel to go up and down the mountain, and the coal for the same run by a steam engine costs £51. In the year when two diesels were substituted for steam, the railway saved £39,000 on fuel costs alone. On top of that, a steam engine needs two men on the footplate, and a night shift has to be paid overtime to keep the fires alight.

There is also the growing problem over coal supplies. Like the other little railways in a land once famous for its coal production, the Snowdon Mountain Railway has great difficulty these days in finding good steam coal. Derek Rogerson is as scathing as the other railway managers about the Russian coal he is having to use.

'It is sold to us as dry steam coal, but really it's just a semi-anthracite.' There was no cheerful sparkle in his eye now, just a cold stare of disgust as he looked out the window at one of the steam trains puffing by. 'The stuff has got such a short flame it just breaks up, and we're showering the countryside with cinders. Look at the roof of that coach out three.' He pointed at its coating of black specks. 'It's a good job the Welsh countryside is so wet...'

Which brought us to the subject of the weather. It is a very crucial factor for a mountain railway. 'We're in a classical feast-or-famine situation. On fine days we can only carry half the people who want to ride, and on other days when the clouds are firmly clamped on the engine shed roof, we have more locomotives than passengers.'

The sparkle came back again. 'People must watch the weather like hawks around here. We can have a bad morning with nobody about and nobody on the roads, the place is deserted. Then the sun comes out, and twenty minutes later the car park is full. Where they all come from so quickly is a mystery to me. They must all be waiting somewhere with their engines running...'

The period of my visit to Snowdonia provided a classic example of the railwayman's dependence on

fine weather. August 9th, 1991, dawned a glorious sunny day. Recovering from the shock, everyone headed for Snowdon. At seven in the morning there were several hundred people milling about in the railway forecourt, even though the ticket office did not open until after eight. Some had come from as far afield as Aberystwyth, 80-odd miles away. By 11.30 every seat for the day had been booked, even though extra trains were added. About a thousand people had to be turned away; it was an all-time record.

For those who did get a ride, it must have been a fabulous experience. As the train climbed the mountain they could look down into the deep valleys and across to the great ranges of mountains on either side, with a distant glimpse of the summit ahead. They could see across the broad sweep of Rocky Valley, and the dark green expanse of Beddgelert Forest, and then far below them a dramatic view of Llanberis Pass. At Clogwyn Station, three-quarters of the way up, they could see the Menai Strait far to the north-west, and the distant peaks of Yr Eifl against the sea. And finally, on the summit itself, the very roof of Wales, they could look down on all those other peaks which had seemed so imposing on the way up, and there were the lakes of Glaslyn and Llyndaw, a deep blue-green because of the copper deposits they lie in, and the ranges of mountains stretching away to the horizon. Across the Irish Sea they might have just glimpsed the outline of the Isle of Man, and perhaps the Wicklow mountains beyond.

A breath-taking panorama, unsurpassed in Britain, and quite unforgettable. So they tell me...

Overnight the clouds came down, the heavens opened, the rain fell. Visibility was negligible, and Snowdon was very, very wet. Yet even on a day like that, 372 people paid to go up the mountain. Derek Rogerson is constantly amazed.

'Sometimes I wonder if there's been a mass break-out from the local psychiatric hospital; any minute I expect people to turn up in white coats with butterfly nets.'

I waited 24 hours for the weather to improve. It didn't, and according to Derek it wasn't going to. He had seen a 'window', up the Pass, a square light in the sky caused by a particular combination of wind and cloud, which old quarrymen had told him was a sure sign that the bad weather had set in. Even so, there was a sizable huddle of escaped patients waiting for the next train, and I decided to join them.

Now you might think it was only the eccentric English who would pay quite a substantial sum to sit on a modestly-upholstered seat in a fairly cramped carriage for the best part of two hours, just to be pushed into a thick bank of cloud and brought back down again. Not at all. We had a Chinese family and an Indian couple on board, and Derek Rogerson told me that the Japanese are particularly keen.

'Mountains are very much part of their culture, and they never had any equivalent of the Victorian engineering era, so they are quite fascinated to see Victorian trains rattling about, and when the trains go up a mountain, that really switches them on!'

The trip was not quite as frustrating as I had expected. We had an excellent view of the spectacular waterfalls of Ceunant Mawr, and the train obligingly stopped for passengers to take photographs _ the Japanese would have appreciated that. As we climbed into open sheep country we could still see across the valley, though a more impressive sight to me was the track ahead, rising quite as steeply as anything I had seen on a fairground, but we were chugging up it without apparent effort. Oh yes, we chugged. It was a diesel engine pushing us, but I hadn't even noticed before. I must have been one of that market survey's unobservant 85 per cent.

We passed a work-train waiting on the loop at Hebron Station – which is not a station at all really, just a convenient passing-place, and not much to do with Hebron except that the building by the track was once a Nonconformist chapel. But on a fairly featureless mountain the timetable compilers had to seize on any landmark.

When we reached the mountain path which crosses the railway just above Hebron the visibility was still a

Opposite: *A pause at Clogwyn Station before the final haul to the summit.*

The red and cream carriages of the Snowdon Mountain Railway at Llanberis, the base station.

few hundred yards, and we could not avoid the scornful eyes of the frightfully fit walkers who were getting to the summit the hard way. We met them later in the summit cafe, and it was easy to tell who had walked and who had ridden. The former were very wet, very sweaty, but enormously smug; the latter were not at all wet and not at all sweaty, but enormously shamefaced...

For the final third of the climb, however, conditions were equally frustrating for walkers and passengers alike. We ran into cloud in Rocky Valley, and from then on we might have been travelling through Surbiton in the fog. Instead of the magnificent views of mountains and valleys and distant sea, all we saw was a blanket of mist, a few yards of rock, and the neck of the passenger in front.

It was a similar story on the summit. The cafe could have been in Piccadilly Underground station for all we could see out of the windows; the only difference was the row of shelves along one wall for the back-packs of the hardy hikers. The view from the platform outside

was no better, and a lot wetter; and few of us lingered there for long.

The cafe was manned by students making a few bob during the vacation, and on a fine day it must be one of the most spectacular workplaces in Britain. Some of them live up there throughout the summer, perched on a mountain-top like the prophets of old, except that the prophets did not have to cope with a train-load of trippers every half hour. They also didn't have to cope with the unpredictable weather. It is rather like a marine climate up there, with a touch of salt in the air, blowing in off the sea. The sky can be quite clear, then there's a slight increase in the wind, a slight drop in the temperature, and with the help of an incoming tide the cloud can roll in and envelope the summit in minutes.

I gathered from the students that it can be quite depressing up there if the cloud stays for days, and coming down into the valley for their weekly break is like returning from outer space. On the other hand, they kept telling me how marvellous the view was on a fine day, and I really should have come up a couple of days before. They cheered me up no end.

The weather is so unusual on Snowdon that there are times in the season when even the most devoted Japanese tourist cannot ride to the summit, even if he is prepared to. In theory the railway starts operating in mid-March and continues daily until the beginning of November. In practice the trains don't get to the summit on a regular basis until about the middle of May, and it gets a bit spasmodic again during October. The problem is not the cloud; visibility is not that important when you are driving an engine at five miles an hour along a track which may look precarious but is actually ultra-safe. What can stop the trains are snow and ice, which clog up the teeth of the rack and even block the track.

There is also the hazard of high winds. That doesn't mean there's a chance of a carriage being blown off the track, even by a force-12 gale. Experiments have shown that it takes a wind force of 68 miles an hour to make even an empty carriage try to roll over, and the

Right: *The loco sheds at Llanberis where steam and diesel jockey for position.*

Below right: *Trains end at Clogywn if the weather is bad.*

force would have to be much stronger if the carriage were full. But the situation is never allowed to arise, because the trains stop running if the wind reaches force-8, anywhere up the mountain. Force-8, around 40 miles an hour, is when a person's individual stability can be affected, and as Derek Rogerson puts it; 'Who wants to get out of a train and be blown flat on your face?'

Even so, people still protest to him when they can't get a ride because of the wind, though they'd protest still more if they did go up, and came a cropper. It's not all fun, running a mountain railway. On the other hand, it has one curious compensation which is shared by all his thirty-seven permanent staff (another 30-odd workers are taken on during the season). They get privilege cheap-rate tickets on British Rail, because the Snowdon Mountain Railway is the only surviving member of the Railways Clearing House, the central body which used to operate when the national railway network consisted of a great many independent companies.

In those days, when passengers bought a ticket for a journey involving more than one company's track, the job of the Clearing House was to work out what proportion of the ticket money went to each company. 'There used to be a famous journey from Inverness to Penzance,' Derek Rogerson told me, 'which involved thirteen sets of different companies' metals. Every quarter they had a massive sort-out – 'you owe me this and I owe you that' – and at the end of it all they just shuttled around a few pounds.'

Closures, amalgamations and finally nationalisation put an end to the Railways Clearing House, but Snowdon's thirty-seven railwaymen still travel at cut rates on British Rail, and in theory, I suppose, the entire staff of British Rail could turn up at Snowdon and demand the same. With the emergence of railway preservation societies, British Rail has agreed in some

Opposite: *The early morning provision and staff train returning to Llanberis.*

Diesel power out of Halfway Station.

cases to make similar arrangements, but none dates back to the old Clearing House days.

There is another facet of the Mountain Railway which singles it out from other Little Trains of Britain, the absence of volunteer support, but it does attract great loyalty and devotion among its staff. Elizabeth Hughes, whose father was a quarryman and knew all about that 'window' in the sky, has worked for the railway for nearly a quarter of a century, latterly as company secretary, and she showed me her battered photo album recording all the staff celebrations and anniversaries over the years; they do seem to have had quite a time.

Nevertheless it is a completely commercial, unionised operation, with no voluntary labour, no supporters' group, no subsidies. It has to make a profit, just like any other commercial company. It went through a difficult period in the late Seventies, when it borrowed money to renew worn-out rolling-stock and equipment, and became trapped between high interest rates and high inflation, but that problem has been overcome, and Derek Rogerson explained why. He has the advantage of not having to go out with an empty order book in search of business.

'So long as we don't treat our customers too badly, so long as we give reasonable value for money – and we do try very hard – then every time the sun shines we get a full order book. We have no difficulty getting more than enough people here when the weather's right, and quite a number even when it's not. And I don't think we ever disappoint them so much that they say they'll never come back again. Most people make at least a second visit; they came with their parents, so they come back when their own children are young, and perhaps again when they've retired.'

I suppose I am an example. My parents first took me on the railway fifty-odd years ago, when I was a small boy. I recall it was thick cloud on that occasion too, and I got very cold and a little wet and extremely bored. Yet here I was again, and I still didn't see much, but one day maybe we'll take a grand-child – and one day, if not that time, then the next time, the sun will shine...

So, I suggested, the future of this particular Little Train of Britain seems reasonably safe. Derek Rogerson agreed – but he held up a cautionary finger.

'Don't forget,' he warned, and the sparkle in his eye was really quite dazzling, 'the Snowdon Mountain Railway does have its ups and downs...'

Romney Hythe & Dymchurch Railway

'The trouble is,' said John Snell as he eased himself into one of the snug bench seats in the station buffet, 'the Romney Hythe and Dymchurch is a very fine railway, but it's in the wrong place.'

It was a fine sunny morning in July and at New Romney Station the public address system was announcing the departure of the 10.35 to Hythe, but there was just a handful of passengers on the train and the platforms were almost deserted. The only other people in the buffet were the two ladies behind the counter. I had been advised that most of the traffic started from the other end of the line at Hythe, and the first train from there had yet to arrive, but even so...

John Snell, managing director of the RH & DR, explained what he meant. 'It was all right forty or fifty years ago. The Kent coast was a great draw in those days, but people go further afield now and this part of the coast is very neglected. If this had been a British Railways line, Beeching would have closed it years ago.'

In fact it very nearly did close in 1971, but the efforts of John Snell and the financial backing of a consortium which took it over have kept it going. 'It's been twenty years' hard work, but we've managed to put it, if not on its feet, then at least on its knees.'

The history of the Romney Hythe & Dymchurch has been chronicled many times, not least by John Snell himself in his book, *One Man's Railway*. The 'one man' was John Edwards Presgrave Howey, who not only possessed a surfeit of surnames but also a surfeit of money. He was indeed the guiding force behind the little railway for over forty years, and his name crops

Loco No. 7, 'Typhoon', making its way towards Dungeness.

Opposite: *A double-header with 'Green Goddess' piloting 'Northern Chief'.*

up all over the place, from the pub which was re-named after him outside Romney Station to the little plaque in the ornamental rockery by the signal-box, which records that his ashes are buried there, within a few feet of the line.

But there were other notable characters involved in the early days of the line, the most famous being Henry Greenly, the engineer who actually built it, and his admirers might not entirely approve of that book title. A rather different version of the line's history

appears, for instance, in *The Miniature World of Henry Greenly*; it suggests that the RH & DR was two men's railway, not one – or if there was only one, his name was Greenly.

'It is perhaps not realised to what extent his was the initiating genius of the scheme,' says the introduction indignantly. 'He was responsible for the whole concept, the civil engineering work, the design of the bridges, the buildings, and of the one-third size loco-motives – tasks unaided by other professional engin-

Romney, Hythe & Dymchurch Railway

New Romney Station, New Romney, Kent, TN28 8PL. Tel. (0679) 62353/63256

Route: Hythe – Dungeness
Distance: 13.5 miles
Gauge: 15 in
Service: Daily, end March – end Sept; w/e March and Oct.

After the First World War two racing drivers, Captain 'Jack' Howey and Count Zborowski, decided to build a miniature railway. In 1924 however, before the project had gone far, Count Zborowski was killed while racing at Monza. Howey went ahead on his own, Romney Marsh was fixed as the site of the line, and in July 1927 his 15-inch gauge railway opened from Hythe to New Romney. Two years later it was extended to a station near the lighthouse at Dungeness: an extension in the other direction, towards Sandling, was surveyed too, but not built. During the Second World War the line was requisi-tioned by the army, and because of its strategic position played an important part in the conflict. By

1945 it was very rundown, naturally, but was re-opened only three months after de-requisitioning, the Romney-Dungeness section having been singled. The world's smallest public railway has since run a regular service, though in 1971 it was doubtful whether this could continue. Against a background of mounting losses, it was decided to sell the line. A preservation consortium took over however, and in recent years an extensive pro-gramme of renewals has taken place. Many of the area's children now depend upon the railway to get them to school, and the line now seems to be in a more favourable position to face the future.

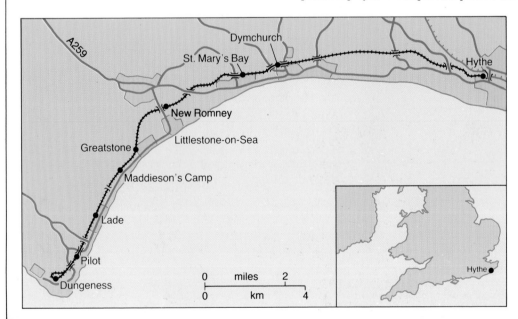

No. 2, 'Northern Chief' 4-6-2 Pacific type locomotive.

eers or architects, and guided only by the dilettante talents of the owner himself, Captain John Howey.'

The authors of this version, I was not too surprised to discover, were Greenly's daughter and son-in-law, so their view is understandable. John Snell's view of Greenly's contribution is rather different. He describes the buildings he erected as 'on the whole, pretty gimcrack and jerry-built', the bridges over the drainage channels in the Marsh were 'none too substantial and designed for a fairly limited life', and the fences alongside the track were 'very poor'. He also notes that after Greenly's departure from the railway, which involved a particularly acrimonious court case, design problems were discovered in his locomotives as well as his carriages.

So Howey and Greenly both have their devoted supporters, which is not surprising because they were forceful characters whose strong views about narrow-gauge railways did not always coincide. However, they managed to work together to create this remarkable miniature line, the first and still the only one of its kind in the world. Howey provided the money and the inspiration, Greenly the technical know-how. It was a formidable partnership between two formidable men – and although it ended in tears, we are still enjoying its legacy.

Neither of these books records the first meeting between them, but they became acquainted through another famous name in the miniature railway world, Bassett-Lowke. Greenly designed model trains for him and Howey was one of Bassett-Lowke's most valued customers, so it was natural that their paths should cross sooner or later. They came from very different backgrounds. Greenly's family had worked on the railways since the earliest days of the steam train, and he himself had a job on the Metropolitan Railway before devoting himself to the small versions. Howey, on the other hand, was the son of an Indian Army

officer who inherited over a million pounds from an uncle in Australia, so he had no need to work at all. His interest in railways came from a friend at Eton, a grandson of the Duke of Sutherland who had the main line built from Inverness to Wick. Howey did not want to build on that scale, but he developed a passion for the miniature variety.

Howey and Greenly first got together to build a 9½-inch railway in the grounds of Howey's home at Staughton Manor in Huntingdonshire. After his father died and he inherited his share of the family fortune he decided to go for something bigger. At that time, 1925, the Ravenglass and Eskdale was the longest narrow-gauge railway in England; Howey wanted his to be longer. Because the Eskdale line has to climb quite steeply the speed of the trains is limited; Howey wanted his to be faster. So he commissioned Greenly to find a site which was level, and straight, and over seven miles long, and a few months later, Greenly came up with the answer: Romney Marsh.

The Marsh in those days was just that, a flat expanse of grazing land depending on drains and dykes to keep it unsubmerged. The ancient Cinque Ports of Romney and Hythe were at opposite ends of it, with Dymchurch the only sizable community in between – 'a quiet scattered village,' one writer described it, 'a delightful place, far from the madding crowd.' The

No. 10, 'Dr. Syn', being turned on the Hythe Station turntable.

Opposite: *No. 10, 'Dr. Syn' crossing Botolphs Bridge with an up train.*

Marsh had the additional advantage, from Howey's point of view, that the Southern Railway had not yet traversed it, and had no great desire to do so. That meant he could legitimately claim that he was providing a public benefit, and thus qualify for a Light Railway Order to carry passengers on a regular basis.

He them embarked on a process which few other narrow-gauge railways have experienced, because most of them run on an existing track-bed, whereas Howey had to start from scratch. The local landowners, the councils, the residents, the bus company, even the local golf club, all had to be approached and convinced that a little railway across the Marsh would be A Good Thing. Interestingly, even in John Snell's rather partisan account, it was Greenly who had to do all the approaching and convincing.

While this process was still going on, Howey managed to buy a field adjoining the main line station at New Romney – which was actually a good half-mile from the town itself. He decided, characteristically, to go ahead with building his own station here, without waiting for any Light Railway Order. It was his land, he argued, and he was entitled to build a station on it,

even if there wasn't any railway line to use it – that was his risk. I doubt that present-day planning officers would go along with that, but in 1925 nobody seemed to bother.

So while a public enquiry was taking place at New Romney, with a consulting engineer condemning the proposed railway as impractical, landowners complaining about their land being carved up, and the secretary of the golf club predicting darkly that the railway would attract trippers 'of the paper-bag and orange-peel variety', just down the road Howey had fifty men building his station. His gamble came off, and the Order was finally confirmed in May 1926 – by which time the station was finished and work had already begun on the line. The first stretch of the Romney Hythe & Dymchurch was opened by the Duke of York, later King George VI, just three months later.

It was quite a short stretch, less than two miles from Romney Station to what is now Jefferstone Lane Station at St Mary's Bay, but at that time it was called Jesson and was close to a boys' camp of which the Duke was patron. He happened to be visiting the camp when that section was completed, and somebody persuaded him to ride on the first train.

Neither John Snell nor the Greenly book says who was responsible for this publicity coup, but I rather suspect it was Howey, because it was he who drove the engine with the Duke on board, and conducted the presentations. Both sources confirm however that this was when relations between Howey and Greenly began to deteriorate, because Greenly was never presented to the Duke, even though he was close at hand throughout the visit.

'Greenly was a proud and touchy man, and was quite shattered by this apparent snub,' writes John Snell. The Greenly book puts it rather differently. 'Greenly's aim in life had never been financial gain, nor the exercise of power, but his Achilles heel was his almost child-like desire to be noticed, and his enjoyment of the praise for his work which was so often his due...'

The line to Hythe was completed a year later, and to Dungeness in the other direction a year after that, thus making a nonsense of what had never been a very accurate name. 'Romney Hythe and Dymchurch' may roll euphoniously off the tongue, but New Romney Station is actually in a seaside suburb called Littlestone; it should have been 'Littlestone Dymchurch and Hythe'. Perhaps Howey thought that sounded more like a firm of solicitors than a railway; certainly 'Dungeness, Littlestone, Dymchurch and Hythe' was never even considered, and as things have turned out he was probably right. Dungeness is best known these days for its nuclear power station, two great concrete hulks set on a vast shingle peninsula, not the most inviting tourist attraction. It shares the peninsula with a couple of lighthouses – as the sea kept retreating they had to keep building new ones, and these are the two most recent – plus a scattering of fishermen's shacks, constructed mostly from old railway carriages – standard gauge, needless to say, not from the Romney Hythe & Dymchurch. There is a wild remoteness about Dungeness which is worth experiencing, even with the power station looming up behind you, and if you can't get enough of it at ground level you can always climb one of the lighthouses, but the train only lingers there for half-an-hour, and most of the passengers were back on board in good time.

John Snell has the right word for the scenery along the route of the Romney Hythe & Dymchurch; he calls it 'low-key'. Between Dungeness and New Romney it is mostly back gardens, and between New Romney and Hythe it is mostly marsh – except for Dymchurch, which is mostly caravans. But this never bothered Howey or Greenly. They were quite happy playing trains, and if the public cared to join in, they were reasonably welcome. 'Commercial viability' did not feature too large in their reckoning. When the Dungeness section was completed, their first thought was not how to make it pay, but who would drive an engine along it first.

Greenly had been on it in the works train during its construction, but he fancied being ahead of Howey in

Engine drivers, Hythe Station.

Operating the points, Hythe Station.

Opposite: *'Dr. Syn' on its final approach to Dungeness Station.*

taking their star loco, *Green Goddess,* along the new track – the Duke of York business was still rankling. The problem was that Howey lived in the bungalow which still stands beside the track at Romney Station, strategically situated between the engine sheds and the new line. To get *Green Goddess* past the bungalow in the early morning without waking him up, Greenly persuaded some of the workmen to push it along the track until it was out of earshot. Then he drove it to Dungeness, and returned in triumph to tell Howey all about it.

This childish rivalry developed into a much deeper resentment a year later when Greenly thought some of his designs were being misused. The Greenly book refers to 'an extremely unpleasant incident' in which he was arrested and brought to court, but it doesn't explain why. John Snell, however, describes how Greenly took some drawings from the office, the work of another draughtsman, and burned them. Greenly claimed they were copied without his permission, and the action was withdrawn. But that was not the end of it; he took out a writ for malicious prosecution, obtained an out-of-court settlement, and ended his association with the railway forthwith.

Howey was out of the country during all this, but he did not seem too devastated by Greenly's departure, and spent the next few years happily removing or altering much of his former partner's work. As it turned out, this period in the 1930s was probably his happiest time with the Romney Hythe & Dymchurch. Regular services were somehow maintained, with the help of students and family friends, who regarded working on a railway as a rather jolly jape; it even made a modest profit for a while. But more than ever it was Howey's personal toy, and he liked to hurtle up and down the line on what John Snell describes as a motorised roller-skate, powered by a motor-cycle engine. 'You pushed it along to start it, and when it fired you jumped aboard before it left you behind...'

Howey and his motorised roller-skate once covered the 8¼ miles between Romney and Hythe in 8¼ minutes. This involved hitting 70 miles an hour on

No. 9, 'Winston Churchill', built by Yorkshire Engine Co. 1931, a 4-6-2 North American Pacific type.

some stretches, and since there were five level crossings on the route, none of which had gates, he was not only risking his own life but that of any hapless road-user whose arrival at a crossing might coincide with his. Fortunately the traffic was a lot lighter in the 1930s, and no casualties were reported.

In another typical escapade he challenged one of his friends to a locomotive race, side by side along the double tracks. The friend happened to be Henry Segrave, twice holder of the world landspeed record, which might have daunted anyone but Howey. But that was in a racing car; Howey reckoned he had the edge on him in a steam engine. So normal service was suspended, and passengers awaiting their train at Hythe Station were confronted by two locomotives hurtling towards them at considerable speed on both the 'up' and 'down' tracks. The locos arrived – and fortunately stopped – simultaneously, and honour was satisfied. When everyone had got their breath back, normal service was resumed, and I imagine

nobody had the nerve to complain about the delay. It was, after all, Howey's railway.

The war stopped the skylarking as well as the normal service, and the Army took over the Romney Hythe & Dymchurch. That area of the Kent coast has always been of military significance, since the days of the Martello Towers. The Duke of York's boys' camp was a first World War Royal Flying Corps station, and at Greatstone there is a wierd concrete structure called a sound mirror which was supposed to detect the approach of enemy aircraft. It didn't do terribly well, but fortunately by the Second World War we'd invented radar instead.

The railway became part of Britain's invasion defences. An armoured train fitted with two Lewis guns and anti-tank rifles trundled back and forth along the coast, on the lookout for enemy armadas. It once claimed to have shot down an enemy aircraft; but Michael Bentine, who is a life-long patron of the railway, maintains that the German pilot mistook it for a full-size train, and thought he was still several hundred feet above it when he flew into the Marsh...

The line was also used to carry the pipes that made up PLUTO – Pipe Line Under The Ocean – which supplied the British forces with fuel after the Normandy invasion. At a more mundane level, it carried the troops stationed at Dungeness into Hythe for their weekly bath. All this varied activity took its toll of the track and rolling-stock, and when the war ended Howey was faced with a formidable repair programme. It took him two years, but when the line reopened it proved an enormous success, in a post-war Britain looking for harmless relaxation. It continued to function profitably until John Howey died in 1963.

His widow put the Romney Hythe & Dymchurch on the market, and successive owners discovered to their cost that it had been running on borrowed time. Howey had reduced repairs and maintenance to a minimum for many years. It was discovered, for instance, that of the six bridges along the route, three needed extensive repairs and a fourth was positively dangerous. There was no stock of spare rail for track repairs, coaches needed rebuilding, engines needed overhauling, the machine shop was falling down. In 1971 it was announced that the railway was being closed down.

Inevitably a campaign was launched to save it; not so inevitably, it succeeded. Richard North, director of an engineering firm, and Sir William McAlpine of the building and construction company formed a consortium which in due course bought the railway for something over a hundred thousand pounds. At that time John Snell had left his job with British Railways, disgusted by Beeching's cuts and the government policy behind it. 'Beeching and Marples between them thought they were going to close down the entire system. 'Who wants trains, they're out of date, let's get rid of them'. Marples may have been a good contractor, and quite good at growing wine, but he wasn't much good as a Minister of Transport!' So John Snell studied law, qualified as a barrister, and was just looking for chambers when the new company was formed. He became managing director – and he has been there ever since.

That was how I came to be sitting with him in the station buffet on that morning in July. He is a genial, expansive character – had he gone into chambers he might have rivalled Rumpole – but perhaps because he was about to visit the dentist, he was in slightly sombre mood. He was particularly gloomy about local planning and development.

'There are still some fine old town centres in the Cinque Ports, when you can find them under all the modern excrescences, and the Marsh churches are still there, but it would be nice if something could be done to turn this part of the Kent coast back into the Garden of England again. It's been very insensitively developed over the last forty of fifty years. It really is squalid, most of it, very squalid indeed – and all the planning legislation has done is put a seal of approval on all the nasty things that would have happened anyhow.'

He shook his head in disgust, and to take his mind off it I asked him about his staff. The Romney Hythe &

No. 8, 'Hurricane', 4-6-2 Pacific type loco in LNER blue, with an up train on the Dungeness turning circle.

Left: *A replica of the world's only 15'' gauge World War II armoured train.*

Opposite: 'Dr. Syn' *pulling out of Dungeness Station with the nuclear power station in the background.*

Dymchurch is manned almost entirely by paid employees, about twenty-five throughout the year and fifty during the summer. In the earlier days many of them were ex-British Rail, but now he is happy to recruit and train his own young drivers for both the steam locos and the diesels. There is no particular preference for steam: 'A lot of the young chaps in their twenties would never have known main-line steam anyway.'

So far as the passengers are concerned, the diesels are actually winning the day. 'The diehard steam buff doesn't think they're an attraction, and certainly steam is a very powerful draw; we still have eleven steam engines. But times are changing. To the youngsters a diesel is a *real* engine. They glance at the steam locos and they say, 'Oh yes, Dad likes them, and Grandpa, but you can't take them seriously'. When they grow up a bit they begin to see that both have their charm. Steam will always be a draw, but a different kind of draw, more of an antiquarian than a nostalgia thing. Young people who have never known it can't be nostalgic about it; it's just curiosity.'

We were getting gloomy again. I congratulated him on the model railway exhibition at the station, a splendid layout with trains starting and stopping automatically, all controlled by a system of magnets. It could well be the main attraction for passengers at New Romney, because the station is set in a suburban shopping arcade on a busy main road, ten minutes' walk from the town in one direction and the beach in the other. The site of the old British Rail station across the way is now an industrial estate. The atmosphere outside the station is not exactly festive; and John Snell agreed.

'Half our business these days is people coming down from London or somewhere else, just for the day, to ride on the railway. A lot of the others are people from all over England and all over the world, who've come here because they've heard of the railway. If we weren't here, nobody would come here.'

So do they get any help from the local authority?

'The District Council paid most of the cost of our first diesel, because they realise we put something into the area, but there's no other subsidy. We run a school train for about two hundred children right through the year, but that's entirely on a commercial basis.'

It occurred to me that this round-the-year operation was the reason why every carriage had a roof, as protection from the winter weather; so many little railways only operating in the summer have a large proportion of open 'toast-rack' coaches. But John Snell explained – very patiently, considering how obvious it was – that the roofs were not just because of the weather, but the bridges. Unlike narrow-gauge railways which have taken over standard-size tracks, the Romney Hythe & Dymchurch bridges are only just high enough to take the small-size carriages; any passenger who stood up at the wrong moment in an open carriage would literally lose his head.

Actually they are not intended to be entirely weatherproof, and not many people expect them to be. 'A woman did write to me recently complaining that she didn't enjoy the ride because it was a cold wet day, and why did we run the train when it was raining? She wanted her money back.' For the first time in our conversation, John Snell chuckled. 'I have to say she didn't get it.' Then he subsided again. 'But it has been a rotten summer so far.'

It was a reminder of the thin numbers around us, and it prompted me to ask about the future of the line. If things didn't improve, was there any prospect of closing down, and this time with no hope of a rescue? John Snell seemed to be expecting the question.

'One doesn't want to close it; one has proved one's credentials in the last twenty years, and one's ability to keep it going. *But...*' – he paused to choose his words – 'looking into the future, if the district continues to turn into a sort of coastal slum, it's going to be more and more difficult.'

Then came the bombshell – to me it was, anyway. 'We've been looking for quite some time at the prospect of picking up the whole thing and putting it down in a better location. Of course it would be a major undertaking, and it would ruffle a few feathers,

No. 7, 'Typhoon', pulling into Dungeness Station.

Opposite: *The up train on the Dungeness turning circle.*

I was still digesting this thought when a distant whistle heralded the arrival of the first train from Hythe, and John Snell perked up. 'This is the train to judge things by. If there's nobody much on this, it's probably going to be a bad day.'

We went out onto the platform and waited for the train. I don't know if he had his fingers crossed, but I certainly crossed mine. And it was not in vain. As the train came into sight I could see all the heads peering out of the windows, and when it stopped, a happy crowd of passengers poured out. Most of them headed for the buffet; the usual group of Japanese enthusiasts ran along the platform to take pictures of the engine. Suddenly New Romney Station had come alive.

We both relaxed. John Snell positively beamed. 'People still come here, you see, if not in the numbers they used to. They pay more money in real terms, and they take longer rides. It's still a worthwhile experience.'

I got the feeling that the Romney, Hythe & Dymchurch was not going to be moved away just yet. And as John Snell went off, almost cheerfully, to meet his dentist, it dawned on me that the name of the railway had a familiar metre. My English master had taught me about metrical feet, but that was too long ago to remember the right name for this one; was it a dactyl or an iamb, or a spondee? But the pattern of the syllables was quite distinct: *long*-short, *long*-short, *long-long* – *Rom*ney *Hythe*-and *Dym*church.

You may have recognised the rhythm already. Captain Howey may have recognised it himself when he insisted on that sequence of names. It fits the last line of a chorus which seems to me highly appropriate, and perhaps Howey was humming it when he drove the first train out of New Romney Station in 1926. McAlpine and North may have echoed it in 1971 when they brought off their successful rescue operation. And I like to picture John Snell leading the chorus when he has found a way of securing the future, yet again, of this remarkable little railway:

'Hooray, up she rises; hooray, up she rises; hooray, up she rises – Romney Hythe and Dymchurch...'

because a lot of people can see nothing wrong with the present situation. The railway is here and the railway's got to stay here, and that's the only thing they can see, but if its roots are being strangled, if its surroundings are deteriorating, it does seem very much better to think about putting it somewhere else, where it could survive more healthily. One way or another we are going to keep it going, but it may be increasingly difficult to keep it going here.'

This sounded pretty revolutionary stuff, and I was tempted to telephone every newspaper I could think of. The Romney Hythe & Dymchurch no longer in Romney, Hythe and Dymchurch? It was only later I discovered that he had said much the same thing in 1983: 'The railway and its assets, its atmosphere, and its traditions are worth keeping; but it cannot be kept unless it can earn its keep, and it could be kept elsewhere. The people of the RH & DR are determined to maintain the railway as a world-famous main line in miniature; and if it is not possible to do so on Romney Marsh, then on another and better site...'

Ffestiniog Railway

'*Merddin Emrys*', *passing Tanygrisiau Reservoir.*

T HE sound came echoing eerily along the mist-enshrouded platform, a prolonged, melodious note, sounding in the distance like a ghostly foghorn.

'OO-OO-OO-OORR...'

It came closer, and a little more distinct. Extra syllables emerged around the central, continuous note. 'In-OO-OO-OO-ORR-unforinOO-OO-OORR...'

It might have been a Victorian street-vendor crying his wares, or Harold Steptoe out totting, or even Pavarotti on a bad day. It was only when the uniformed figure passed the train window that the words became quite distinct.

'Min-FFOOORDD...Anyone for MinFFOOOORD...'

Hamilton Sparks, housemaster at Charterhouse School, enthusiastic amateur operatic singer, and volunteer guard on the Ffestiniog Railway, waved to the driver of the venerable engine at the head of the train and climbed back on board, as we set off again on the climb to Blaenau, seven hundred feet above.

Hammy Sparks, as he is universally known to fellow volunteers, teaching colleagues and pupils alike, was just what we all needed. It was a damp, dreary, depressing day, with a mist coming down from the mountains and a drizzle coming in from the sea, and Porthmadog had been looking its worst. The traffic moved even slower than the bedraggled holiday-makers on the pavements, and by the time we had found a parking space there was only a moment for a quick greeting before we tumbled aboard the 10.45. And we had only just disposed of our damp coats, and caught a glimpse of the grey sea as we crossed the Cob, the great embankment which blocks the estuary, when we stopped at Minffordd Station. All I could see through the mist on the deserted

Ffestiniog Railway

Porthmadog, Gwynedd, LL49 9NF. Tel. (0766) 512340

Route: Porthmadog (Harbour) – Blaenau Ffestiniog
Distance: 13.5 miles
Gauge: 1 ft 11½ in
Service: Daily, end March – beginning Nov; limited winter service.

In 1836 a narrow-gauge tramway, its gauge decided by that already in use in the quarries at Blaenau Ffestiniog, was built to carry the slate from those quarries to the nearby estuary. The gradient was skilfully engineered so that slate trains could travel down by gravity, the wagons being pulled back up the hill by horses. By the 1860s the growth in traffic was making such a slow method of working uneconomic, and steam haulage, with a consequent increase in capacity, began in 1865. It continued until 1946, though the line went through a difficult period in the 1930s, as a result of which the passenger service ceased in September 1939. Freight was carried throughout World War II, but on 1 August 1946 this was discontinued and the railway abandoned. Then, in 1951, inspired perhaps by the example of the Talyllyn, just down the coast, a revival began and the first length of line was re-opened in July 1955. Gradually, section by section, the railway was extended, despite the immense problems which had to be overcome – getting past the hydro-electric scheme's reservoir above Dduallt (The-altht) was but one of them. Finally, on 25 May 1982, passengers re-entered Blaenau Ffestiniog by the narrow gauge for the first time for nearly 43 years.

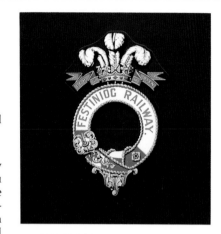

'Earl of Merioneth' *steaming into Minfford.*

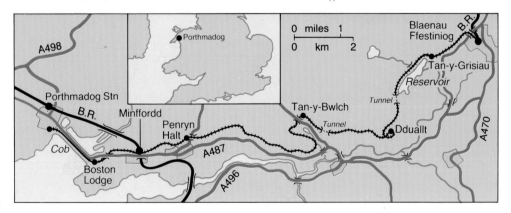

platform was a painted sign announcing: 'The Coming of the Lord Draweth Nigh'. Then came that wierd, ullulating cry, and for a heart-stopping moment I thought that the lone figure emerging from the gloom might be the advance party for the Heavenly Host. But it was Hammy Sparks who drew nigh, a comforting figure in his railway guard's uniform, and we were grateful for his company, not only at mist-enshrouded Minffordd but whenever he could spare time from his duties during the rest of the journey. As a result I was able to get a wealth of information about the line from someone who had worked on it as a volunteer for twenty-eight years, first in the station shop, then on the buffet car, then as a signalman and guard – and still so devoted to it that he spends a fortnight each year travelling up and down the track, three times a day each way...

Our conversation was punctuated, of course, by those musical performances at each station. His rendering of 'Anyone for Tanygrisiau' was particularly impressive, but I cherish the hope that one day at Tan-y-Bwylch, which is the station for Llyn Mair Lake, he'll try it to the tune of 'Danny Boy'. 'It's Tan-y Bwylch, the lake of Lynn Mair's ca-a-lling...'

The reason for these musical announcements, incidentally, is not only because Hammy likes to ham it up. (I am surprised that nobody at Porthmadog has re-christened him the 'Corn' on the Cob.) 'If I just shouted the names of the stations,' he explained to me simply, 'I'd be hoarse by the end of the day. So I sing them instead.'

He also gives a running commentary to the passengers over the public address system. Yes, the trains on the Ffestiniog have public address systems – it's that sort of railway. And I soon learned that it has many other features which make it unique among the Little Trains of Britain, and the doyen of all narrow-gauge railways.

Like many other Welsh railways, the Ffestiniog owes its existence and its survival to the English.

Right: 'Merddin Emrys' *on the 'Cob', Porthmadog.*

'Merrdin Emrys', *a double-Fairlie loco, shunting at Porthmadog Station.*

Blaenau Ffestiniog were still sending their slate down to the coast on pack animals or in carts. It was another Englishman, a Worcestershire engineer called James Spooner, who was brought in by the quarry owners to survey and build a railway line down the mountainside. In 1832 the Festiniog Railway Company – spelt the English way – was incorporated by Act of Parliament. That makes it the oldest railway company in the world still operating; it was the first of a series of 'firsts' which the Ffestiniog has achieved over the years, each of which is a piece of railway history in itself – as anyone who works on the Ffestiniog will not fail to tell you...

Spooner found that the Cob, which Madocks had built to keep the sea out of the estuary, provided a useful track-bed for the final mile into Port Madoc. It was rather like the flat section at the bottom of a children's slide, because the slate waggons came rolling down the line just by force of gravity, and if they got out of control, the level stretch across the Cob could have slowed them down before they hit the buffers. Everything depended on the intrepid brakeman, who careered down the mountainside on one of the waggons, hauling on the brake as they took the steep curves, and hoping to goodness he could stop them at the bottom.

It would have added an extra dimension to the job if he had to keep them rolling across the Cob itself, knowing that if he braked too hard they would stop too early and he'd have to get out and push, but if he braked too gently they wouldn't stop at all, and he'd finish up in the harbour. Alas, no such luck; the old prints show that on the final lap the waggons were pulled sedately across the Cob by a couple of horses.

A third horse – the one that drew the short straw, as it were – actually rode on the waggons too, no doubt keeping its hooves crossed that the brakeman knew what he was doing, and with the depressing knowledge that if they got down safely, it would have to pull the empty waggons all the way up again. Life for a horse on the Ffestiniog in the early days must have been very much like flying is today; five per cent

Indeed Porthmadog itself, where the railway starts, is the creation of an Englishman, William Alexander Madocks, MP for Boston in Lincolnshire. Madocks was a land developer and speculator on a grand scale, rather like another Englishman, John Corbett, who later turned the inland town of Towyn into a seaside resort, the headquarters of the Talyllyn. But while Corbett converted a rural coastline into a profitable housing estate, Madocks converted a tidal estuary into a profitable rural coastline.

It was he who built the Cob across the mouth of the River Glaslyn in 1811, thus creating a new harbour and reclaiming a vast acreage of rich arable land. The harbour was called Port Madoc, but like so many Welsh names (Towyn is now Tywyn) the spelling has been confusingly altered on the maps and is now Porthmadog. That distances it from Madocks, but no amount of name-juggling can alter its English origins.

It was not Madocks, however, who thought of the railway. When he died in 1828 the quarries around panic, and 95 per cent boredom – with hard labour thrown in.

Spooner built the railway to a gauge of 23$\frac{1}{2}$ inches, wide enough for the horse to walk up the middle and narrow enough to get round the curves. That was less than half the width of the early standard gauge railways, and too small, it was thought, for a steam engine. But Spooner's son Charles, who took over the railway in 1856, liked the idea of steam-power to haul the increasing quantities of slate; no doubt the horses liked it too. In 1863 two little locomotives were delivered, the first of their kind, and a year later, as the result of another bright idea from Spooner, the Ffestiniog notched up another 'first' – it was the first narrow gauge railway in Britain to get permission from the Board of Trade to carry passengers.

To begin with, people travelling on the Ffestiniog had almost as uncomfortable a ride as those now-redundant horses. They sat back-to-back on wooden seats in open carriages, and told not to move about too much in case it tipped over. But at that stage most of

'Earl of Merioneth' *being prepared for its next train at Boston Lodge.*

Left: 'Earl of Merioneth' *returning along the 'Cob' to Porthmadog.*

Hopefully not a portent of the coming train journey.

Hunslet-built 'Linda' 2-4-OST at Tan-y-Bwlch Station.

Opposite: *Porthmadog-bound, 'Earl of Merioneth' passes Campbell's Platform.*

the passengers were quarrymen employed by Spooner, so nobody argued. Anyway, it was better than clambering up the mountain on foot.

By 1869, with four engines, a bigger workforce and lots more slate, Spooner got an Act passed which permitted the line to be doubled. I'm not sure why he bothered, because he immediately decided it would be too expensive and plumped for more powerful engines instead, to pull bigger trains. But they still had to negotiate those tight curves, and so along came another Ffestiniog 'first' – the push-me-pull-you double-bogie engine designed by Robert Francis Fairlie to go round corners. It looks for all the world like two engines back-to-back, with the cabs in the middle and a chimney at each end. It doesn't actually bend in the middle; the bending is done by the swivel bogies at the front and back. These days the same principle is used on most diesel and electric locos – but the Ffestiniog saw it first...

Fairlie's bogies came to be used on the passenger coaches too, which gave the railway another 'first'. It still has in service the earliest bogie coaches in Britain – not the height of comfort to ride in, perhaps, but steeped in history.

Where the Ffestiniog led, standard gauge railways followed – literally. Two of them turned up at Blaenau Ffestiniog, the London & North Western from Llandudno and the Great Western from Bala. At the other end of the line, on the coast, the Cambrian Railway arrived from the south. Railways in fact were springing up all over the countryside, much as golf courses are today. It was flattering for the Ffestiniog, which had set the example, but also very galling, because the slate could now be taken away by train from Blaenau on these other lines without any need for push-me-pull-you engines or swivel bogies.

When slate fell out of fashion in the 1920s, only the passenger traffic was left to keep the Ffestiniog going, and most of those passengers were tourists. When the second World War broke out, even the tourists disappeared. The Ffestiniog struggled on with what freight traffic it could find from the quarries, but it wasn't

enough. When the quarries stopped for the August holidays in 1946, the Ffestiniog stopped for good.

This was when the railway's first 'first' became a liability. The Act which permitted it to be created in 1832 made no provision for it to be dismantled. The thought of it closing was never contemplated at that time: 'What Parliament has joined together, let no man put asunder...' So although the Ffestiniog stopped functioning, it continued to exist, and all the track and rolling-stock just stayed where it was.

It took steam enthusiasts five years to wake up to the plight of the railway, by now in a state of advanced neglect and deterioration. Just for once it failed to achieve a 'first', but it did come a close second to the Talyllyn in the history of railway preservation societies. The first meeting was held in Bristol in 1951, just a few months after Talyllyn supporters held their first meeting in Birmingham. Three years later a Trust was set up to hold the shares of the railway company, and in deference to the original spelling – as well as reflecting its own English origins – it was named the Festiniog Railway Trust. The two spellings still exist: the same office at Porthmadog Harbour Station sends out letters from the Festiniog Railway Company and the Ffestiniog Railway...

So began the most astonishing era in the history of the railway. Nearly every preservation society has had to struggle with overgrown track, worn-out engines, decrepit rolling-stock and derelict equipment, but the Ffestiniog chalked up another 'first', and it has yet to be matched. It is the only little railway to have had part of its track submerged under a reservoir by the British Electricity Authority.

Up until then the restoration work had proceeded in the conventional way. A passenger service was resumed across the Cob, just as far as Boston Lodge, where the engineering works were located; Madocks had used the same site as his own works depot and named it after his constituency. A year later the line was opened to Minffordd, then to Penrhyn and Tan-y-Bwylch in 1958. But by then it was obvious there was no way the old line could be re-opened all the way to

Blaenau. The Electricity Authority had brushed aside all protests and obtained a compulsory purchase order to acquire and flood the last section. The railway, it seemed, would only get as far as Dduallt, just below the reservoir; it was another three miles to Blaenau Ffestiniog, and most of it would be under water.

But the true railway enthusiast will not be thwarted by the odd reservoir. An alternative route was devised and surveyed, involving a spiral around Dduallt with the line curling over itself to gain the necessary height above the reservoir and rejoin the old track. Typically, it was another 'first'; the first and still the only spiral of its kind on any narrow-gauge railway in Britain.

It would involve carving out two miles of entirely new line through some of the most difficult and inaccessible terrain in Wales, but in 1964 they decided to go ahead and build it. And it would be built, as the official guide simply puts it, 'with largely volunteer labour, no money and no plant, across land they did not own.'

Happily they were given the land, the money was raised and the plant acquired. But here's the interesting bit. It was not the railway enthusiasts, on the whole, who provided the labour, it was an entirely different type of volunteer who was not particularly interested in railways, but very interested indeed in creating a new route through virgin territory in Britain's equivalent of the Australian outback or the African bush. It was the chance to be pioneers, not too far from their own doorsteps – a chance never likely to occur again. It was another Ffestiniog 'first'.

The new stretch of line was called the Deviation, and those who worked on it were called Deviationists. That sounds like some wierd religious sect, and certainly the folk you speak to on the Ffestiniog these days seem to regard them as a people apart. Hammy Sparks, for instance, was around when the line was being built, but when I asked if he had been a Deviationist himself he seemed ever-so-slightly shocked. And Gordon Rushton, now general manager of the Ffestiniog, agreed that the pioneers were fast becoming a part of local folk lore.

'Different activities attract different people. They just happened to get a kick out of building a railway in the middle of nowhere...'

It conjures up a vision of hairy men in big boots and red check shirts, with an axe in one hand and a stick of gelignite in the other, and no doubt there were one or two Deviationists who met that description – or liked to think so. But they were actually drawn from all walks of life, just like the more orthodox railway volunteers. They included, for instance, groups of Crusaders, the Christian youth organisation, who made it their regular annual camp.

Some of the pioneers stayed to work on the railway, but once the job was done, most of them went off in search of more mountains to conquer. These days I expect they are using up their energies on sponsored walks...

The spiral at Dduallt and the new Moelwyn Tunnel were completed in 1977, and the Ffestiniog claimed yet another 'first' – the largest civil engineering project in Europe ever carried out almost entirely by voluntary labour. But there was still much work to be done to restore the last stretch of the existing line beyond the spiral, and link up with the new. It took another five years, then in May 1982, the 150th anniversary of the original Act of Parliament and thirty-six years after the line closed, the first train made the complete journey again from Porthmadog to Blaenau Ffestiniog.

From the windows of the carriages the passengers could see then, as we can now, the old line disappearing into the waters of the reservoir as they started climbing the spiral, then see it emerge after they reached the top. In their nightmares, no doubt the train took the wrong turning...

So that was that. The whole line was operating again, the job was done. What now?

'We were quite confused in 1982,' Gordon Rushton confesses. 'We'd achieved what we'd been trying to do for twenty-five years – to make the Ffestiniog run to Ffestiniog. We had opened the last section of line after

Right: 'Earl of Merioneth' *heading towards Tan-y-Bwlch*.

the Deviationists had completed theirs, we had got compensation from the Electricity Authority, we had become a statutory authority with grants from the European Community, we'd arrived in Blaenau in style. Now we had to adjust from reconstructing the railway to running it. There was a great backlog of maintenance, the stations were tatty and had to be refurbished, the locomotives and carriages needed re-painting – some were rotting away. But the great thing about the Ffestiniog is that our chief lubricant is enthusiasm and our greatest fuel is goodwill.'

He quoted that metaphor twice while we were chatting, and I suspect he has used it many times else-where. It is a great marketing slogan and Gordon Rushton is a great marketing man. When we met he had only been general manager for a week: at the age of 45 he had decided to give up a job managing one of Sealink's shipping lines, specialising in leisure market-ing, to work fulltime for the railway on which he had been a volunteer for twenty-five years, on the foot-plate, as a guard, and more recently as chairman of the Railway Society.

He took over at a good time. The compensation he mentioned from the Electricity Authority was £106,000, which went a long way towards all the out-standing maintenance and repairs. The help from Brussels was substantial too; it provided a new carriage shed at Porthmadog, a new station awning at Blaenau, and the means to start building another of those distinctive double-engines, now the loco logo of the Ffestiniog. An item like building a new steam engine would present a massive financial problem for most little railways, but in the boardroom at Porthmadog, I gather, the main headaches were not over how to pay for it, but what to call it and what colour to paint it.

The volunteers were an even bigger asset than the grants, providing a third of the workforce at any one time, equivalent to a substantial and on-going subsidy. As for attracting the customers, even on the wet day of my visit, with the marvellous views from the train reduced to a few hundred yards of soggy hillside, they

Opposite: 'Merddin Emrys' *climbs towards the line's summit, near Tanygrisiau.*   **Above:** 'Merddin Emrys' *at Dduallt Halt.*

were packing them in at nearly ten pounds a time for the round trip.

Given such a healthy situation it must be tempting for a new general manager to sit back and let things puff along. But as well as all that financial support which other little railways might envy, there comes a weight of responsibility on Gordon Rushton which they might not envy at all.

'We take our trains up and down the mountain at the maximum peak performance of the locos, and we have to perform professionally and efficiently, because we have British Rail at either end and our own cus-tomers in the middle. So we've got obligations. We're not just pottering through the countryside from point A to point A-and-a-bit.'

And I must say this does affect the atmosphere of the Ffestiniog, compared with all the other narrow-gauge railways I have visited. It was reflected in the luxury of my first-class compartment with its smart blue upholstery emblazoned with the railway's

97

Opposite: The down train hauled by 'Merddin Emrys', leaving behind the slate tips of Blaenau Ffestiniog as it approaches Tanygrisiau.

insignia, in the service provided by the girls from the buffet car, coming along the corridor with trays of refreshments, in that public address system with the running commentary...

I had to look out of the window and see the more venerable carriages along the train and the push-me-pull-you at the front, to remind myself that I wasn't on board a miniature Inter-City.

Hammy Sparks had emphasised the difference too. 'The Ffestiniog has always been much busier than the Talyllyn, for instance, and the number of passengers we carry nowadays is very large. The Talyllyn is a marvellous railway, but compared with the Ffestiniog it's just a branch line.' He added hastily – 'but none the worse for that.'

But hadn't some of the fun gone out of it, I asked him, and Hammy agreed that in the earlier days it had been more personal, with fewer people involved so each volunteer played a bigger part. But he still enjoyed it: 'There's the additional attraction of being part of a very professional and slickly operated machine.'

Gordon Rushton took much the same view of the status of the Ffestiniog, though he preferred the term 'provincial express' to Inter-City. 'We have three little halts where people can stop us on request – you hardly get that on an Inter-City.'

He agreed there were different reasons why people enjoyed themselves working on the Ffestiniog compared with the earlier days, but they still did – or they wouldn't come. With a thousand volunteers on his books, I could hardly argue. Then he explained why.

'People react to different situations. People who like organisation and running a railway come here, people who like doing lots of hole-digging and pioneering go to the railways which are still developing. Not all our volunteers are dotty about steam. They may not be railway enthusiasts particularly, but they like the Ffestiniog because their friends come here, and there's a good social life, and the scenery is marvellous. Oh yes, they like trains too – but that can be secondary.'

There is certainly one feature of the Ffestiniog which would not appeal to the fanatical steam buff. The familiar smell is missing, the smell that comes from the smoke of a coal-burning fire. The reason is simple; engines on the Ffestiniog burn oil. The Forestry Commission and the insurers insist on it, because much of the line passes through dense woodland, and even in the Welsh climate there would be a great risk from the sparks.

Gordon did not have too many regrets. 'We do miss the smell a bit, but we console ourselves that oil gives a much better performance, like having a turbo on a car. The heat is more controllable and much better, and you can switch it off when you want to. It makes it easier for the fireman too; those cabs on the Fairlies are pretty small, and when you're firing coal your backside sticks out the side – you're very exposed!'

Oil is also much cheaper, the way the Ffestiniog gets it. 'We have a network of volunteers around the country, watching out for bargains in waste oil. They pick it up and bring it here, in anything from 45-gallon drums to pint tins, and we process it, blend it with diesel oil, centrifuge it, get it exactly as we want it, then fill the locos with it.'

There are diesel engines too, but they are only used on the first and last trains of the day, because although not every volunteer is a steam enthusiast, they cater for passengers who are. 'If a father tells his kids they're going to see a steam engine and they don't, his credibility suffers something rotten.' But there are some modern coaches like the one I travelled in, to cater for the Philistines – and Gordon explained how it came about.

'We had put together a train where everything was over a hundred years old. In America each of those coaches would have been put on a plinth, but here they were, still running around on the railway. We were all standing there proudly admiring them, and along comes a passenger and he says...' and Gordon assumed a devastating Birmingham accent – 'This train's terrible, all these little compartments – I can't get a drink!'

He shed the accent. 'Well, it won't do if you've come all the way from Birmingham and you can't get a drink. So we mix them up a bit now.'

We talked about local involvement. Among the volunteers on other Welsh railways I sometimes found it hard to find a Welshman, but perhaps because the Ffestiniog offers scope for other activities too, it seems to attract more support from the locals, particularly families. Gordon himself is not Welsh and he has no family – 'I suppose I'm married to the Ffestiniog!' – but he was born not far away on the Wirral and went to school in Colwyn Bay. Now he's become a local resident himself, he's anxious to encourage more local participation – and one way he is achieving it is through the Parks and Gardens Department.

I imagine this was another 'first' for the Ffestiniog. It started off modestly, with a few volunteers tending the flowerbeds and the grass at the stations, but now it is doing up buildings as well. A locally-based couple, Eileen and Neil Clayton, one a lecturer at the Snowdonia National Park Centre and the other an engineer at the hydro-electric station, have drawn in local families to help them, particularly youngsters. Gordon Rushton has a marketing man's term for it, kid-power, and he has good reason to be proud of it – his own office had just been entirely re-decorated for his arrival by twelve and thirteen-year-olds, and it had been done as professionally as everything else on the Ffestiniog.

'If adults take children seriously instead of just saying, "Oh, they're only twelve, they don't know anything yet", then you can bring out their latent enthusiasm and show what they're capable of. And through this kid-power we can tap into other local families – the English kids have Welsh friends, and they get their families interested too. By the time they're sixteen they know our system and the people who are running it, and they're able to walk straight into a volunteer's job without any problem – so kid-power is generating us new volunteers.'

These family links can extend, I discovered, from near-the-cradle to the grave. The local Warner family, Trevor and Maggie and their three sons, were all volunteers, but the week before my visit Maggie had died of cancer, and Trevor suggested they might use the old hearse waggon, which had been parked in the sheds for years, to take her ashes up the line to be scattered. Everyone had agreed, and the waggon was at that moment being checked over in the workshops. *Prince*, one of the original 1863 engines, was to be dressed overall in black crepe, and on the footplate would be two of Maggie's sons, David and Robert. *Prince* would take the hearse waggon and the funeral party up to Tan-y-Bwylch, and the ashes would be scattered there.

'It's not macabre, it's how it should be, for someone who loved the railway.' Gordon Rushton smiled – as indeed he mostly does. He is a very cheerful man. 'You'd be amazed how many other people have come up to me and said they'd like to make their last journey like that, at least a dozen of them – and I've only been here a week.'

Yes, it has to qualify. Another 'first' for the Ffestiniog...

Opposite: 'Linda' *hauling the up train behind Barlwyd Terraces near Blaenau Ffestiniog.*

'Linda' *approaching Blaenau Ffestiniog, passing old slate miners' cottages.*

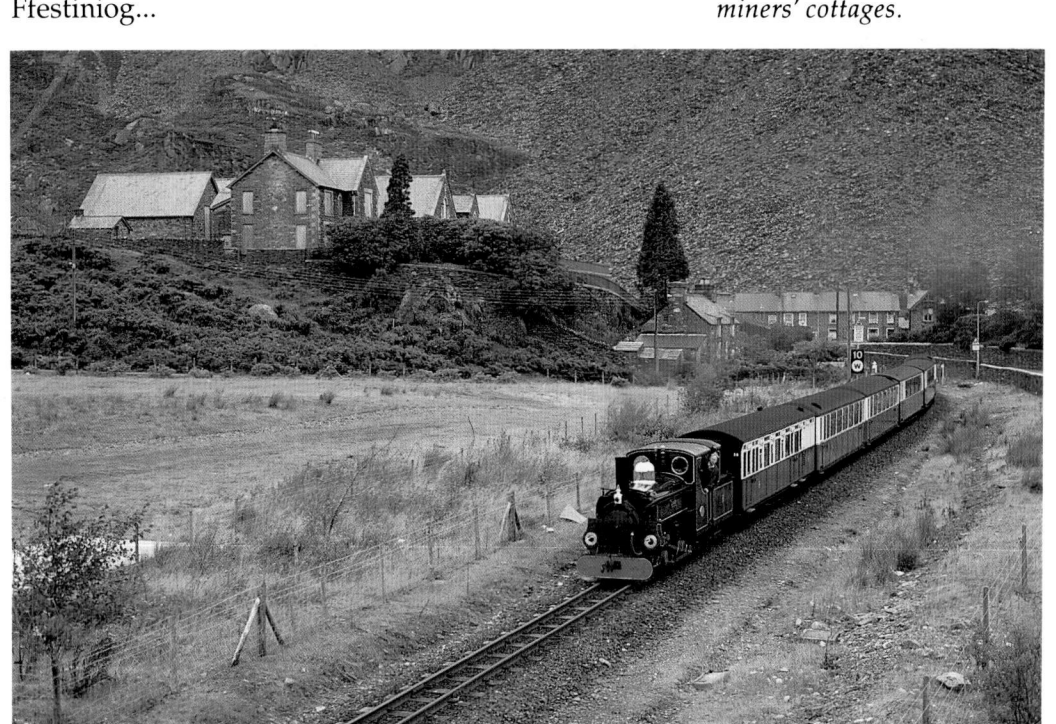

Sittingbourne & Kemsley Light Railway

EVERY narrow-gauge railway likes to have some distinctive feature which no other railway can match. It may be the steepness of its gradients or the sharpness of its curves, the antiquity of its engines or the freshness of its buffet sandwiches. It may even claim some sort of record: 'The Loveliest...', 'The Longest...', 'The Highest...' – perhaps even 'The Smartest...', though I doubt they'd be allowed to get away with that.

The Sittingbourne & Kemsley Light Railway, tucked away in an area of North Kent which is part-industrial, part-suburban, and part-nothing-in-particular, faces something of a quandary in this respect. It does have a rather unusual viaduct which might excite devotees of reinforced concrete, but until now it hasn't dreamed up an appropriate superlative to put on its brochure. May I therefore tentatively suggest that it calls itself the MUESLI Line – not only because it provides simple, healthy enjoyment for a great many people, but because it is the little railway which has 'the Most Un-Exciting Surroundings- and Loves It!

The SKLR rather reminds me of the flowers which used to bloom on derelict bomb-sites after the war; there is an irrepressible spirit of cheerful determination about it which transforms its unromantic setting. If that is too fanciful a comparison, then how about re-adjusting SKLR to BKLR, the Bisto Kids' Light Railway. There may be smuts on its nose and its cap may be slightly askew, but it is enjoying itself hugely.

To reach it you park on a stretch of sunken waste ground, not unlike a bombsite itself. You hear an encouraging hiss of escaping steam round the corner, but when you get there you find it is escaping, not

'Premier' on its return trip through the Kent marshes.

Sittingbourne & Kemsley Light Railway

Sittingbourne, Kent.

Route: Sittingbourne – Kemsley
Distance: just under 2 miles
Gauge: 2 ft 6 in
Services: variable – enquiries to Mr M Burton, 85 Balmoral Rd, Gillingham, Kent, ME7 4QG. Tel. (0634) 52672

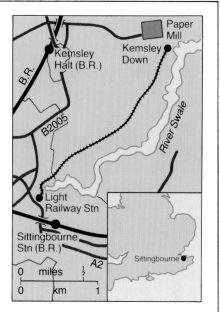

The first part of the railway was opened in 1906 to carry paper from a wharf on Milton Creek, Sittingbourne, to the mill – two of the three engines bought to run the line then, *Premier* and *Leader* are still at work on it today. Later the line was extended to a wharf at Ridham, on the river Swale, a total distance of about four miles, to allow the import of logs and woodpulp. Later still, when after the First World War the demand for newsprint grew to unprecedented levels, a new mill was built about halfway along the line, at Kemsley. From 1923 the line served the new, modern mill continuously for 24 hours a day, even throughout the Second World War, without a single failure that could be laid at the door of the railway, until the mid-60s. Then road transport took over the job of the railway, but since the Company did not wish to see the line die it arranged with the Locomotive Club of Great Britain (LCGB) to take over, on loan, the two miles of track between Sittingbourne and the mill. From 1 January 1970, the LCGB formed a light railway section to maintain and operate the line, a duty now performed by a separate Company, whose members are all members of the Railway Society.

Standard gauge loco 'Bear' on display at Kemsley Down.

Opposite: *Bunker-first 'Premier' approaches Kemsley Down.*

from a steam engine but from a huge pipe alongside the footpath. It looks like a dangerous leak, but nobody seems too bothered, and it will still be hissing away when you return.

Ahead there is a daunting flight of wooden steps up a steep bank, and having scaled it you find yourself surveying, from this elevated vantage point, an array of rubbish dumps in the foreground, and beyond them, like a concrete forest, line after line of massive concrete pipes, lying on their sides or standing on end, almost obscuring the factory which manufactures them. You also find yourself alongside the booking-office of the Sittingbourne & Kemsley Light Railway.

The line is just two miles long, and it runs between two paper-mills, each of them representative of the square-box school of industrial architecture. Any steam which has failed to escape from that pipe down below is coming out of the chimneys. The first half-mile of track runs down the concrete viaduct to ground level, and underneath it is a semi-permanent encampment of travellers, who seem to have over-looked the official rubbish tips a few yards away and, when I was there, were steadily creating their own.

The next landmarks alongside the line are a sewage works and a car breaker's yard, but it does reach open country at last, a stretch of marshland with a distant glimpse of water, The second mill, however, is already getting close, and it is difficult to ignore the steam pipe which runs alongside the track, hissing away menac-ingly in the long grass and every so often ejecting a plume of steam into the air...

There is no mistaking, in fact, that the Sittingbourne & Kemsley was an industrial railway. During its working years there was no pretence at landscaping, or even tidying up, and when the owners had no further need for it, only the most devoted light railway enthusiast could have dreamed it would be any use for anything else. But happily there is no shortage of devotion and enthusiasm where little railways are concerned, and out of this unpromising length of track has been created the most popular tourist attraction in the area, carrying over ten thousand passengers a year, with an annual turnover from fares, sales and subscriptions of more than £30,000 – and it has all been done by voluntary effort.

When Edward Lloyd Ltd built the first section of the railway in 1906, to carry paper from a wharf on Milton Creek to the mill at Sittingbourne, they could hardly have foreseen this reincarnation. They would certainly not have believed that two of the three engines they bought to haul the paper would still be working on the line nearly ninety years later, hauling people – nor that those people would have come from all over North Kent just for the ride.

'Triumph' *carefully negotiates the concrete viaduct out of Sittingbourne Station.*

In those days the area must have looked even less inviting. From the mill at Sittingbourne the track had to twist and turn through rows of back-to-back houses, and beyond them was the 'dark flat wilderness of a marsh' which Charles Dickens had in mind when he wrote the first chapter of 'Great Expectations'. You remember how young Pip first saw the escaped convict looming out of the mist, 'a fearful man, all in coarse grey, with a great iron on his leg, a man with no hat and with broken shoes and an old rag tied round his head, a man who had been soaked in water, and smothered in mud, and lamed by stones, and cut by flints, and stung by nettles, and torn by briars, who limped and shivered and glared and growled...'

The folk who walk the marsh these days are rather more presentable, but even today it is not too difficult to visualise just such an apparition emerging from the high grass, and ninety years ago it must have been quite eerie to drive the little trains along this track, especially if there was a mist coming up from the estuary. They must have been quite glad to reach the wharf – though Milton Creek is not exactly welcoming if the tide is out and the mud is exposed to the nose as well as the eye...

During the first World War the line was extended another two miles past Milton Creek to Ridham, on the River Swale, where the trains picked up supplies of logs and pulp. It meant that drivers had twice as far to travel across the marsh, and twice the chance of seeing strange figures looming up through the mist, limping, shivering, glaring, growling...

The isolation of that stretch of marsh is difficult to picture these days, because in 1923 the company built its second paper-mill beside Milton Creek, and the very un-rural 'village' of Kemsley grew up around it. It forms the limit of the present track, so you are never out of sight of a building throughout the run, but if you only look in certain directions, and ignore that ubiquitous steam pipe, it is quite possible to imagine that you are in the country.

But that isn't the point of the SKLR. 'This isn't one of your Ffestiniogs or your Talyllyns, this is an industrial railway. You don't get the fancy scenery here.' Thus said Malcolm Burton, chairman and general manager, and the guiding genius behind the whole project ever since the line was taken over from the Bowater Group in 1969.

Bowaters had bought up Edward Lloyd in 1948, and for the next decade they continued to improve and expand the railway, until in the late 'fifties there were thirteen steam locomotives operating on the line, and up to four hundred carriages and waggons. The line not only carried freight but took Bowater employees to and from work – and as they worked day and night shifts, the trains kept running day and night too. But in 1965 the company was advised by time and motion experts that it would be more economical to transport men and materials by road, and with the example of Dr Beeching to follow, they reluctantly agreed. They decided however that it would be nice to preserve at least a part of the line, and in the years that followed they liaised with the Association of Railway

Preservation Societies, and through them the Locomotive Club of Great Britain. The chairman of the Locomotive Club was Malcolm Burton.

At that time Malcolm was still working for the Southern Region of British Rail at Waterloo Station, 'diagramming' trains and staff. That meant allocating locomotives and rolling-stock, and rostering drivers and guards – not a far cry from what he has done over the years, on a rather smaller scale, for the SKLR. Like so many railwaymen, his spare time was bound up with railways too, and it was he who led the Locomotive Club team which negotiated with Bowaters. On October 4th, 1969, a ceremony was held to mark the official handover of the line, with every available locomotive in steam to whistle agreement. Under the agreement the line was loaned to the Club for a peppercorn rental of one pound a year.

During the next six months the members salvaged all the track they required from the unpreserved stretch of the line between Kemsley and Ridham

Left: *'Triumph' 0-6-2ST built by W.G. Bagnall in 1934.*   **Above:** *The shunting of carriages at Kemsley Down.*

Dock, helped by Bowater cranes and lorries. They selected the rolling-stock they wanted, and dismantled entire buildings for re-erection at their new headquarters. The biggest of these was a transit shed four hundred feet long and sixteen feet high, made of steel and corrugated iron. One of the SKLR's brochures describes the operation in suitably dramatic terms:

'The wind and snow howled across the marshes as the faithful carried frozen sleepers and frozen corrugated sheets, and huddled round the stove in the old weigh-bridge, which had been made available as a frontier post until surrendered to the forces of the developers.' All that was lacking was the figure of an escaped convict looming out of the marsh...

Meanwhile Bowaters were clearing a site behind the Kemsley mill for the line's headquarters. At the

Sittingbourne end of the track, which now stopped short of the other mill, the coaches were being given a new coat of green paint, and the locos were being serviced in the engine shed, which was due to be removed as soon as the one at Kemsley was erected. It was all a desperate race against time and the developers, but on Good Friday, 1970, the target date, the locomotive *Premier* burst through a banner of newsprint, hauling the first trainload of passengers from Kemsley to Sittingbourne. They were the first of six thousand passengers who travelled on the SKLR in that first season.

To start with, the railway operated on a membership basis, but at the beginning of 1972 a limited company was formed and Malcolm Burton gave up the chairmanship of the Locomotive Club, to concentrate all his efforts on running the Sittingbourne & Kemsley.

Tom Wilding, who was chairman of Bowaters at Kemsley, is still president of the SKLR, and although the company had a management buyout a few years ago and now calls itself UK Paper, the relationship between them and the volunteer railwaymen remains very amicable. This is perhaps just as well, because the railway is still very much linked to the mill complex at Kemsley, and there is no public access to the line at that end, except by train. That is why all passenger journeys have to start and finish at Sittingbourne, but because all the engine sheds are at Kemsley, that is where the line has its headquarters, its refreshment room and its museum. In fact the only buildings at the Sittingbourne end are the booking-office, which even by booking-office standards is not exactly commodious, and the sales kiosk, which is much the same.

This set-up can create a curious situation, because I was meeting Malcolm Burton at the Kemsley headquarters in the morning, and the trains didn't start running until the afternoon. The only way to reach him was through the security system at Kemsley Mill, which at that time, after a number of unexplained fires and other vandalism, was very secure indeed. I had to be vouched for, and issued with a pass at the main

Paper mill steam pipes crossing Sittingbourne Station.

gate, then walk round the inside perimeter fence, past the gruesome machines which extract the gubbins from the papermaking process, through a high wire gateway which is normally kept closed to keep out any stray passengers, underneath an arch of the ubiquitous steam pipes, around the engine sheds and sidings – and into an astonishing rural oasis in the heart of this industrialised desert.

When the SKLR took over this site it was a wasteland, overgrown and derelict, the papermill's grubby backside. Bowaters cleared it and the railway volunteers laid out a grass area with chairs and tables overlooking the creek. They built office accommodation and a refreshment room, installed a couple of static locos on the grass to provide the proper railway atmosphere, and set up a little museum inside a caravan. Coming upon this unlikely haven after negotiating the seedy environs of the mill was impressive enough; to passengers arriving after their two-mile ride past the rubbish tips, the pipes factory, the sewage

Opposite: 'Triumph' *passing the steam pipes that feed the UK Paper PLC paper mills.*

farm and breaker's yard and the marshy wilderness, it must look like the Promised Land.

It was here that I heard Malcolm's story, sitting at one of the tables drinking coffee in the sunshine, while the waters of Milton Creek lapped gently beside us – mercifully concealing the low-tide mud – and the familiar smell of a coal-fired steam engine wafting from the sheds, where they were getting steam up for the afternoon runs. After thirty-eight years with British Rail he had taken early retirement in 1988 to give the SKLR his undivided attention.

'Operating a preserved railway is a bit different from running the Locomotive Club. They're both to do with railways, of course, but with this you've got to have a different sort of professionalism. Safety, management, accountancy, budgets, a board of directors...'

He paused in his daunting list of responsibilities to tackle a more basic management problem, as a call for help came from the refreshment room. 'All right, Gran, I'll give you a hand with moving the chairs back. You carry on in the kitchen.'

Gran, he explained, was Mrs Baker, the mother of the catering manager, Margaret Embleton. She was 76 years old, but most weekends she travelled the fifty-odd miles from her home in Hythe to help out in the refreshment room, because her daughter had to combine her catering duties with being a senior nursing officer at the local hospital, and she was a divisional officer in the St John Ambulance Brigade as well. Another member of the family, Ian Embleton, would be on duty in the sales kiosk at Sittingbourne.

This, I discovered, was typical of the SKLR. The line is very much a family affair, for those who operate it as well as those who come to ride on it. The reason for Gran's chairs being out of place was a family celebration the previous evening, an engagement party for one of the members. And there was evidence all around me that these family links could last for life. One of the carriages in the sidings was named after George Sticker, who was a vice-president of the railway until he died at the age of 84; it had been dedicated by his widow, who at 85 was still acting as mem-

Driver of 'Premier' loco, 0-4-2ST built by Kerr Stuart in 1904.

Opposite: 'Premier' *pulling out of Sittingbourne Station.*

bership secretary. And next to us on the grass was a table and garden seat presented by the family of Peter Blackburn, another loyal supporter who had died tragically early at 56.

The youngsters were in evidence too when the line opened for business, boys and girls helping their parents to cope with the influx of passengers. The whole operation had the atmosphere of a cheerful family outing, and that atmosphere must be contagious, to attract so many thousands of visitors each year to this unpicturesque corner of Kent. Sittingbourne, now part of Swale Borough Council, is trying hard to be a tourist area, and indeed Malcolm Burton is vice-chairman of the Swale Tourism Association, but Swale also includes Faversham, with its picturesque Tudor market place and four hundred listed buildings, and Sheerness, with its traditional seaside entertainment. Not even the Swale tourist brochure can find much left to say about Sittingbourne.

Even in the days of King Alfred, Sittingbourne must have been less than enchanting, because the king much preferred neighbouring Milton and conferred regal status upon it. Today, in the midst of the universal red brick that submerges them both, you can still find a Tudor Court Hall in Milton Regis, whereas Sittingbourne is dominated by one of those modern council offices designed to be functional rather than picturesque – its only attempt to look decorative is the bright yellow paint on the handrails outside the main door.

The fine old parish church still stands across the road, but it is flanked these days by a freezer showroom, and although there is a 'farm shop' in the High Street, it all seems a long way from any farm. My only pleasant surprise was the Old Oak in the middle of the one-way system, a pub with an uninviting exterior which proves to be as deceptive as its name – the Old Oak is in fact a sailing barge, not a tree. Inside I found a landlord wearing a collar and tie, which on that hot summer Sunday was a great rarity in Sittingbourne, and beyond the bar a tiny back garden with a really dazzling display of herbaceous borders

Coupling the carriages to loco 'Triumph' at Sittingbourne Station.

how the refreshment room had been broken into a few weeks before, by smashing a window and tearing a safety wire. On other occasions there had been thefts of loco parts from the engine sheds, and damage to the buildings. It may seem curious this could happen when there is so much security at the front of the mill, but the railway area is outside the main perimeter, and the barbed-wire fence which divides it from the marshes and the creek has been cut almost as fast as it is erected.

So vandalism and theft are two of the immediate problems for the Sittingbourne & Kemsley, though steps have since been taken to make its headquarters more secure. In the long term, the main worry must be that feature of the railway which they are so proud of because of its rarity if not its beauty, the half-mile viaduct out of Sittingbourne. It was built in the 'thirties, one of the first concrete viaducts of its kind and probably the only one in Britain used by a narrow-gauge railway; they like to tell you so, anyway.

It is not exactly in the same class as the Ribblehead viaduct, that magnificent line of lofty arches which carries the Settle-Carlisle railway across the Ribble Valley; this is just a series of crossed concrete supports which carry the line from the little wooden terminus at Sittingbourne, between the rooftops along the Milton road on one side and the upper slopes of the Council rubbish tips on the other, down to the sewage farm at ground level. Many a Philistine might regard it as an unprepossessing structure in unlovely surroundings. But to the members of the SKLR it is a thing of beauty and a joy – they hope – for ever.

It looks sturdy enough, and it is inspected regularly, but if it ever needed major repairs they would be far beyond the resources of the Sittingbourne & Kemsley. Malcolm Burton is under no illusions. 'We have no bank loans, nothing to mortgage, we can only spend what's coming in. We do have a reserve fund for extra expenses like repairing a boiler, but that's it.'

So the train takes things gently on the viaduct – not that it breaks any records elsewhere. 'We keep to 15

and hanging baskets and decorative pot plants, a very welcome and colourful refuge in the heart of the congested town centre.

But that sort of haven takes some finding in Sittingbourne. Its most attractive feature, the cynics might say, is the road that leads out of it. Yet people pour in from Maidstone and Whitstable, from the south London suburbs and the camping sites on the Isle of Sheppey, and yes, even from picturesque, photogenic Faversham, to have a ride on the Sittingbourne & Kemsley Light Railway. They continued to come when attendances at other preserved railways dropped during 1991 by fifteen to thirty per cent. Malcolm Burton can quote all the figures because he is also secretary of the Association of Independent Railways...

Alas, there are other kinds of visitors as well. The isolated area behind the paper-mill where the SKLR has its headquarters may be ideal for an engagement party, but it is ideal for vandals too. Malcolm told me miles an hour, partly for safety and partly to save on wear and tear, but anyway it's no good rushing people up and down. They've come to enjoy the ride, after all. We could belt from one end of the line to the other in about eight minutes if we wanted to, but it'd be highly dangerous – and anyway, there'd be no point.'

The speed limit on the viaduct is five miles an hour, and only one engine is allowed on it at a time. Having taken that precaution, Malcolm and his colleagues can only keep a wary eye open – and their fingers crossed.

They were in a happier position with their rolling-stock. When they took over the line there was quite a range to choose from, and the sidings and sheds still seem to be full of engines and carriages, albeit in various stages of dismemberment and repair. The official stock list shows seven steam locos and two diesels, as well as three standard gauge locomotives acquired from other railways, just to put on show. They have a number of coaches from the old Bowater stock, and four from the former Chattenden & Upnor Military Railway on the Isle of Grain.

Chattenden and Upnor are no great distance from Sittingbourne and Kemsley, just a dozen miles across the Medway as the seagull flies, but the carriages travelled hundreds of miles to get from one line to the other. They were bought first by the Welshpool and Llanfair Railway and went off to Wales in 1963; the SKLR bought them fifteen years later, and brought them all the way back again. In their military days they were open-sided, and the troops they carried were simply ordered not to fall off. Now two of them have been converted to closed coaches and the other two are fitted with doors, for the safety of less well-drilled passengers.

Three of these coaches, the *Chattenden, Lodge Hill* and *Four Elms*, named after the stations on their original line, were part of the train I travelled on from Kemsley to Sittingbourne, but I was up in front of them, in the company of Alan Corthorn and John Hindle, driver and fireman of *Premier*. This is the jolly-looking green and black engine with the two big circular windows which has been trundling up and

'Premier' *being shunted into position for its return trip to Sittingbourne.*

down this track since 1906.

The SKLR has a gauge of two feet six inches, and after riding in the 10¼-inch *Hero* on the Wells & Walsingham, *Premier* seemed very nearly a full-size engine. There was a reasonable amount of room for all three of us to stand alongside, though it was just as well that John did not have much stoking to do, because it would have meant manoeuvring the shovel through my legs. The cab is quite a height above the platform, and I could understand at last how superior it must feel to be a real engine-driver. I could also understand why they always wear caps; it took only a few minutes for my hair to be full of smuts. Any lingering sense of superiority soon wore off when John opened the firedoor and a blast of heat enveloped our legs; this really must have been a most uncomfortable way of making a living.

Yet Alan and John were doing this voluntarily, and obviously enjoying it immensely. John was a comparative newcomer; he had only moved from Surrey two

Yet another 'Thomas the Tank' *engine!*

The guard, for instance, Terry Mann, is also a relief fireman, editor of the railway's newsletter, and thanks to his rotund figure he stands in for Father Christmas on the Santa Express. He actually earns a living driving a fork-lift truck, but even that has a railway connection – he works for Hornbys, makers of model trains.

I rode with him for a while in his guard's van, and admired his blue uniform with the SKLR lapel badges and buttons. It turned out he had adapted it himself from an old blue suit. It was his own idea: 'You can't do this sort of job in a T-shirt and trainers!' I discovered that, apart from its decorative value, it adds a little more authority when he has to warn youngsters on the marsh to keep clear of the train as it passed. But he told me he had a difficult time on one occasion dissuading some children from trying to ride on the buffer beams between the carriages; it required much activity with his red flag and whistle to sort them out.

In spite of their occasional failings, though, Terry enjoys the company of children on the train. 'I'd rather do this than be an engine-driver; it's more fun among the passengers. The only time I get bored is when we don't have any.'

He had no chance to get bored on this run. It was Teddy Bear Day, when any child accompanied by an adult and a bear travels free, and word had obviously got around. The train was absolutely packed with parents and children and cuddly toys. Instead of running the usual hourly service the train shuttled back and forth continuously throughout the afternoon, to the great delight of Alan and John, who got twice as many rides on the footplate as they had expected, and to the even greater delight of Tony Nokes, a bank clerk with Barclays and voluntary commercial manager and booking clerk for the SKLR.

Malcolm Burton was very gratified too, having completed his furniture-moving duties in the refreshment room and now acting as station announcer at Kemsley. And so was David Vannerley, a director of the railway company in charge of publicity and marketing, resplendent today in his stationmaster's

years before. But Alan had known the line since he was a boy, when it was still operating for Bowaters. In those days, he recalled, as John jumped down to couple *Premier*, the couplings were rather more primitive – they were known as 'shunter-crushers.' In 1964, when he was fifteen, he was allowed into the sheds to look over the engine, and it must have hooked him as firmly as those couplings, because when the line was taken over he was one of the first to join the new company.

He started as a fitter, became a fireman in 1975, then graduated to driver, under the tuition of the SKLR's senior driver, Tommy Farr – not the boxer, but a British Rail driver who divides his time between the SKLR and the main line from Euston to Manchester. As well as driving *Premier*, Alan is chairman of the locomotive committee, and the engineer responsible for the boilers, and fits in a fulltime job with GEC Avionics. This assortment of duties is not unusual on the Sittingbourne & Kemsley; nearly everyone seems to double up on jobs, except for those who triple up.

uniform, adapted from British Rail surplus stock. He started on the SKLR in the engine sheds, 'wearing overalls and big boots and doing what I was told' – which must have been quite an experience for a teacher of religious education at Canterbury High School...

It was a highly successful day, part of another successful season, but there is still much to be done on the Sittingbourne & Kemsley. They are hoping, for instance, to provide a better service for disabled visitors. The steep steps up the bank to the Sittingbourne platform require a fair amount of fitness, and even a push-chair can be quite a haul. At present they make special arrangements for a disabled persons' coach to be admitted through the Kemsley mill security system.

There are also long-term plans to have a station halfway along the line, as part of Swale Council's programme for turning the marshes into a leisure area; that would certainly be invaluable if the concrete viaduct ever decided to call it a day. And there is a lot of work still needed on the locos and rolling-stock. When I was there, for example, they only had one engine functioning – its normal companion was in the sheds with a nasty case of worn-out tubes.

But even within its present limitations there is no doubt at all that the Sittingbourne & Kemsley is a source of tremendous enjoyment to a great many people. It offers entire families a jolly, companionable afternoon's entertainment in the most unlikely surroundings. And that's just the people who run it...

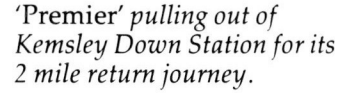

'Premier' *pulling out of Kemsley Down Station for its 2 mile return journey.*

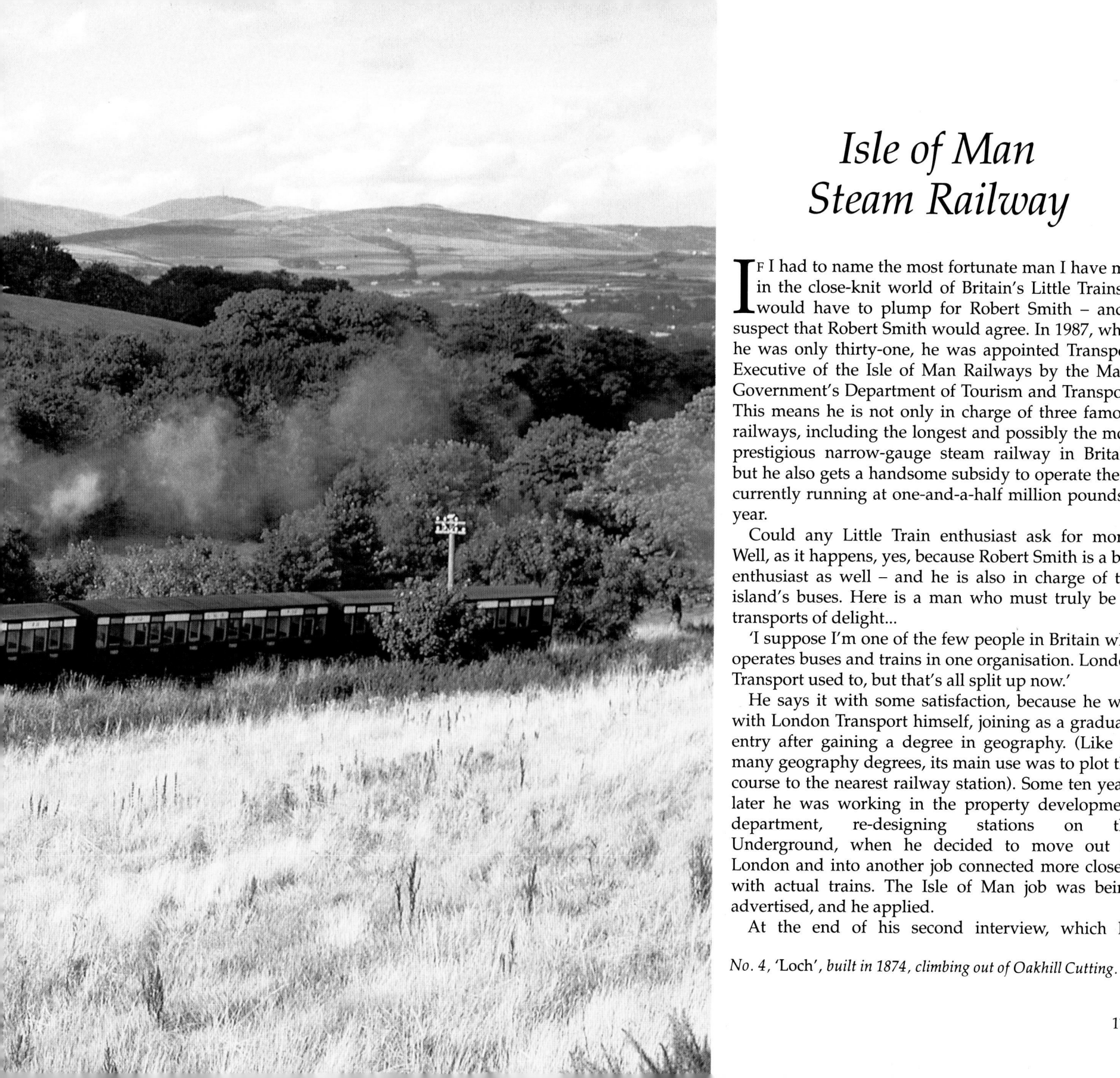

Isle of Man Steam Railway

I F I had to name the most fortunate man I have met in the close-knit world of Britain's Little Trains, I would have to plump for Robert Smith – and I suspect that Robert Smith would agree. In 1987, when he was only thirty-one, he was appointed Transport Executive of the Isle of Man Railways by the Manx Government's Department of Tourism and Transport. This means he is not only in charge of three famous railways, including the longest and possibly the most prestigious narrow-gauge steam railway in Britain, but he also gets a handsome subsidy to operate them, currently running at one-and-a-half million pounds a year.

Could any Little Train enthusiast ask for more? Well, as it happens, yes, because Robert Smith is a bus enthusiast as well – and he is also in charge of the island's buses. Here is a man who must truly be in transports of delight...

'I suppose I'm one of the few people in Britain who operates buses and trains in one organisation. London Transport used to, but that's all split up now.'

He says it with some satisfaction, because he was with London Transport himself, joining as a graduate entry after gaining a degree in geography. (Like so many geography degrees, its main use was to plot the course to the nearest railway station). Some ten years later he was working in the property development department, re-designing stations on the Underground, when he decided to move out of London and into another job connected more closely with actual trains. The Isle of Man job was being advertised, and he applied.

At the end of his second interview, which he

No. 4, 'Loch', built in 1874, climbing out of Oakhill Cutting.

Isle of Man Steam Railway

Strathallen Crescent, Douglas, Isle of Man.
Tel. (0624) 663366

Route: Douglas-Port Erin
Distance: 15⅜ miles
Gauge: 3 ft
Service: Daily, Easter hol, end Apr – end Sept; not Sats in Apr.

The railway in the Isle of Man dates back to a time, in the 1870s, when suggestions were made that Douglas and Peel should be linked. A line gauged at 3 feet opened in 1873, with a longer, more difficult, route to Port Erin the next year. The expense was prohibitive, and when the Manx Government was asked for financial support for a line to Ramsey, it refused and the scheme was dropped. Not happy about this, the people of Ramsey promoted their own Manx Northern Railway to St. Johns, which was opened in 1879. Traffic remained high on the whole system until the 1950s, but then road transport began to absorb the passengers. Closure threats were rife for some time, the line from St. Johns to Peel succumbing finally on 3 June 1967, and the Douglas-Ramsey route the following year, both lines having been re-opened for a final season after previous closure. Various attempts were made to revive them, but without success. Finally, in 1977, the Manx Government nationalised the railways: the only survivor, the line to Port Erin, has run ever since, rightly making capital from its steam power. A significant number of passengers are local people, while from the visitor's point of view much interest is created by vintage survivors in both locomotive and carriage stock.

Fired and ready, No. 11, 'Maitland', in Douglas Station.

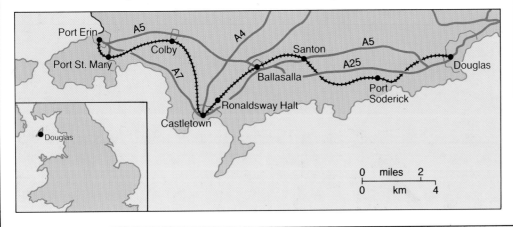

thought had gone rather well, he went to leave the room and walked into a cupboard. When he finally located the right door, he found it was sticking and had quite a struggle to open it. The Board members had been watching with some amusement.

'One of the first things you'll have to do when you start here,' said the Minister, 'is to get that door fixed!'

Said Robert Smith afterwards: 'That was the first intimation I had that I'd got the job...'

So the new young chief executive stepped out of the frustrating large-scale problems of London Transport into the much more satisfying little world of vintage railways. 'It was quite a change from working in a large organisation to becoming the head of a small one, but I feel more in touch here. If I want a job done, I ask one person to do it, and it's done. In London Transport you have to consult Uncle Tom Cobbley and all.'

But the change is much deeper than that. Instead of designing new stations for a modern network, Robert Smith is now dedicated to preserving the most historic set of railways in Britain. One of them, from Douglas to Ramsey, the longest electric tramway in the British Isles, celebrates its centenary with some spectacular festivities in 1993, and the Snaefell mountain railway will then have only a couple of years to wait; but even though they are nearly a hundred years old, they are still the youngsters in the group. The third member of the trio, and for steam buffs by far the most important, is their senior by twenty years.

The Isle of Man Steam Railway is much reduced from its original size. The lines to Peel in the west and Ramsey in the north, and the branch line to the Foxdale lead mines, have long since disappeared. But the 15½-mile line from Douglas to Port Erin in the south is still functioning, and more significantly, it has not resorted to what Robert Smith calls 'Disney-like re-creations' to do so. It is still using some of the same engines and the same rolling-stock it started out with, back in the heady days of the 1870s.

Right: *No. 12, 'Hutchinson', steaming towards Port Erin.*

That was when the island was becoming the popular playground for the North of England. Mill and factory workers from the big industrial cities, finding themselves with the unaccustomed luxury of a week's holiday each year with full pay, escaped from the smoke and grime to enjoy the fresh air and the gentler pace of the Isle of Man. But they only got as far as Douglas; the delights of the old capital of Castletown, and the beaches at Ramsey and Port Erin, and those succulent Manx kippers in the smokehouses of Peel, could only be reached in horse-drawn waggons along rough country lanes. The inhabitants of these other towns were as keen to see the tourists as the tourists were to see them, and an obvious opportunity awaited. The situation was made to measure for a steam railway.

After several false starts, the Isle of Man Railway Company was registered at the end of 1870. Although the islanders were enthusiastic, they were reluctant to back up their enthusiasm with hard cash, and there was quite a struggle to raise enough capital locally. They produced only £30,000 towards the target of £200,000, and it took another two years, with a lot of help from outside, before the first length of track was laid, on the route from Douglas to Peel.

The track has a three-foot gauge, but it might easily have been the nearly-two-foot gauge favoured by some of the Welsh quarry railways. The chief engineer, one Henry Vignoles, visited the Ffestiniog and seemed quite impressed, but according to the reference books he came under the influence of another engineer, Robert Fairlie. Fairlie designed those famous push-me-pull-you engines for the Ffestiniog, but apparently much preferred lines with a three-foot gauge, which he reckoned were more suitable for carrying passengers. He persuaded Vignoles to take the same view, and the three-foot gauge was adopted for the Manx steam railway, the Douglas to Ramsey electric railway, and even the horse trams on Douglas promenade.

Engines were ordered from the Manchester firm of Beyer Peacock – Mr Vignoles just happened to be 'closely associated' with them – and the first one, named after the company chairman, Lord Sutherland, was delivered early in 1873. It was followed in due course by fourteen more, all built to the same design, which made things simpler, not only for the drivers and the engineers who maintained them, but also in much later years for the preservationists, since all the parts could be swopped around.

The old *Sutherland* is now parked permanently in the railway museum at Port Erin, but others like *Loch* (no Scottish connection this time, just the name of the island's Governor at the time), which arrived for the opening of the Port Erin line in 1874, is still working on the same route, one of the oldest steam locomotives in service in the world.

The rolling-stock still looks much the same too, thanks to some loving restoration work by modern craftsmen in the Victorian repair sheds at Douglas, where some of the lathes are still operated by the original overhead belts and pulleys. When Colin Goldsmith, the works foreman, showed me round, it was like stepping back into history; he should really have been wearing an ankle-length overcoat and a stovepipe hat...

Left: 'Loch' *in a scene little changed for more than a century at Santon Station.*

Right: *No. 12, 'Hutchinson' built 1908 and named after a former deputy chairman.*

Red-bricked Douglas Station designed by the noted Manx architect C.H.E. Cowle.

Colby Station is provided with a passing loop, the only one between Castletown and Port Erin.

Swiss cottage-style building, Port Erin Station built in 1903, the southern terminus of the railway.

Opposite: *Waiting for the train at the Ballybeg Halt.*

The only 'modern' stock in the sheds were two diesel railcars, a mere forty years old, which had been bought from a railway in County Donegal in 1961 as works trains. They are still used occasionally, but they are never used by passengers; this is, after all, a vintage steam railway, and it intends to stay that way. The only members of the public who see them are visitors from Ireland who ask to see 'their' diesels. Actually the railcars were only in Donegal for eleven years and they have been on the Isle of Man for over thirty, but the Irish regard the entire island as a piece of their own country, a lump of earth torn out of Loch Neagh by an Irish giant and hurled into the sea, so their proprietorial attitude towards anything on the Isle of Man with the remotest Irish connections is perhaps understandable.

Colin's team were working on the Foxdale coach while I was there, which was used on the branch line to the lead mines in the 1880s. It boasted one superior compartment specially installed for the benefit of the mines captain, who had the privilege of a first-class train pass and would otherwise have been unable to get any benefit from it. The mines closed in 1911, and the Foxdale was put into service elsewhere. And many years later, Colin told me, it was fitted out as a kind of caravanette by Lord Ailsa, the man who came to the rescue of the steam railway in the 1960s. During the TT races and the practice periods he would have it parked in the sidings at Balasalla for his use, so he could escape the noise of the bikes.

Later the coach interior was covered with formica, which was not an improvement. 'It looked pretty tatty, to put it mildly,' said Colin. That has all been ripped out, and the original panelling and bodywork restored, complete with the 'duckets', the little gable windows jutting out on each side of the guards' compartment, so he can duck his head into them and look along the length of the train without getting wet. By now the Foxdale should be back in service on the Port Erin run. Watch out for coach F39, and you may find yourself sitting where the mines captain used to relax in solitary state with his first-class pass. In these more

democratic times, it costs no more than the other compartments.

The Foxdale branch line was originally run by a separate company, and the line up to Ramsey was owned by yet another, the Manx Northern Railway. Perhaps it is something to do with the island's three-legged symbol, but it does seem traditional on the Isle of Man never to have one organisation where three will do, particularly so far as railways are concerned. There are three supporters' clubs, for instance, the Isle of Man Railway Society, the Isle of Man Steam Railway Supporters Association, and the Manx Electric Railway Society. Fortunately they all get along happily together, and with Robert Smith, though it must triplicate the liaison work at the railways' headquarters.

The three-company set-up foundered in 1905. The Foxdale company was hit by the fall in lead production at the mines, the Manx Northern was hit by the competition from the new electric tramway to Ramsey, and eventually the Isle of Man Railway bought them both. Three into one did go, very satisfactorily, and the railway prospered.

In 1913 passenger figures topped the million mark for the first time, and although normal traffic dropped during the first World War, there were plenty of troops to carry instead, when the island became a detention centre for enemy aliens. The railway even had to build a new stretch of line, from Peel harbour to a vast camp at Knockaloe, one-and-a-half miles away, where twenty thousand aliens were detained. In 1917 the passenger figures were up past the million mark again; the ill wind of war had blown somebody some good.

The post-war years were even better, as the holiday-makers returned. In 1925 the figures hit an all-time high of 1,344,620. But then the war clouds gathered again over the Isle of Man Railway; this time the enemy was not the Germans, it was the omnibus. In 1927 Manxland Bus Services, which originated from Cumberland, introduced a fleet of vehicles operating from Douglas to all corners of the island.

The railway countered by increasing the number of trains, cutting fares, and speeding up journey times. It also formed its own bus company to fight the invaders on their own ground, while a group of local bus operators joined in the free-for-all by forming Manx Motors. Yet again, the island had produced three separate bodies to do one job.

And again it was the Isle of Man Railway which won through. It bought out both the invaders and the locals, consolidated its own bus fleet as a subsidiary company, and introduced multi-purpose tickets which could be used on buses or trains. Although individual coach operators still ran excursions, the company now had a firm grip on all the public transport on the island.

The second World War had much the same effect on the railway as the first. The tourists disappeared, the troops and aliens arrived, the trains continued to carry more than a million passengers a year. Better still, it meant the service was needed, not just in the summer, but all the year round, and thousands of 'specials' were laid on too. This time the ill wind blew even better...

When the war ended the magical million continued to be achieved, year after year, as the holiday business boomed. Trains of eight and ten coaches were quite common, carrying up to a thousand passengers in each train. There were eleven or twelve trains a day on the Port Erin line, nearly as many to Peel and Ramsey. Happy days had never really gone away, but they were certainly here again. The directors must have felt that every day was Christmas.

I trust they made the most of it, because they were never to feel that way again. A new cloud was gathering on the horizon, not another war or another bus invasion, but the package holiday. Unfamiliar words like 'Majorca' and 'Tenerife' were creeping into the nation's vocabulary; even Manxmen were taking their holidays abroad.

The turning point came in 1956. That was the last year the magical million was achieved; the holiday-makers from Manchester and Liverpool were now

Opposite: *No. 12, 'Hutchinson', heads a Port Erin-bound train out of Douglas.*

flying further afield. Train services on the island were reduced, some were cancelled altogether. Engines nearing the end of their serviceable life were not replaced. Smaller stations were closed, at first just for the winter, then permanently. By 1963 only one engine was in use throughout the island during the winter, and in the summer there were only six trains a day to Peel and Port Erin, and just two to Ramsey. In 1966 no trains ran at all; the company looked like closing down.

Enter the Most Honorable the Marquess of Ailsa, Earl of Cassilis, laird of Cassilis Castle in Ayrshire – and steam buff extraordinary. He possessed just the attributes the railway needed: a love of steam, and a lot of money. The newly-formed Isle of Man railway Supporters Association welcomed him with relief and delight, and the following year the railway re-opened in a sea of grey toppers and frock-coats (the Governor's party), tam-o'shanters and kilts (Lord Ailsa's party), and general euphoria (everyone else).

The euphoria was not to last long. Nor was Lord Ailsa's enthusiasm, as business failed to pick up. After a year the lines to Ramsey and Peel were closed. The Manx government provided some help to keep the Port Erin line going, but it wasn't enough. When Lord Ailsa's losses reached about £43,000, he announced that he would be giving up his lease on the railway at the end of the five-year option, in 1971. It faced closure again.

The railway company, which still owned it, got together with the Manx government and somehow, for the next few years, they muddled through, running spasmodic services over sections of the line. The company's centenary came during this period, and so did the centenary of the Port Erin line a year later. There were the usual ceremonial trains and commemorative dinners, and a spot of flag-waving here and there, but the celebrations were understandably muted, particularly in Peel and Ramsey, where the tracks had been removed and there were never to be trains again.

It was in 1976, exactly twenty years after the fortunes of the railway had began to slide, that they started being re-built. A newly-elected House of Keys, the island's Parliament, decided that the ad hoc system of making grants to the company was no way, in fact, to run a railway. They decided to buy it instead. In this the Isle of Man, as is its wont, was a little behind the times, but at last it had got the idea: nationalisation.

There was a distinct flavour of Dr Beeching in the way the new management lopped off the inessentials to make ends meet. The platform canopies and booking hall verandah at Douglas Station were removed instead of renovated and the eleven tracks at the station reduced to five, Port Erin platform was demolished, and the station building at Port Soderick disappeared altogether. Some of the carriage sheds at Douglas and Port Erin were shared with the buses, which had been taken over too.

The drastic pruning worked. With the money saved, four engines were made operational, coaches were refurbished, an efficient vacuum braking system was installed, and the track was repaired. The passenger figures for the Port Erin line started to pick up; they passed the hundred thousand mark in 1978 and nearly reached two hundred thousand in 1979. They didn't manage to stay there, but they never slumped below six figures again. When Robert Smith took over in 1987 the line was firmly established again as a tourist attraction, albeit on a much smaller scale than the original railway.

But the main problem still remains: there is no passing trade on the Isle of Man. Some local people do use the railway, to go shopping perhaps in Douglas, but the vast majority of passengers are holidaymakers from the mainland, and the numbers continue to dwindle. It is hardly surprising, when you can fly to the Mediterranean just as cheaply, with rather better odds on seeing the sun. Robert Smith is hoping they can reverse the trend.

'We are going through a period of transition at the moment, trying to attract higher-spending people who are interested in special-break holidays, golfing,

Opposite: *No. 4, 'Loch', ready to leave Ballasalla Station.*

Below: *No. 11, 'Maitland', pulling the Port Erin-bound train near Port Soderick.*

fishing, and of course the railway, so that although the numbers may drop, the actual contribution to the economy increases.'

So if the island is trying to go up-market, why not offer more facilities on the trains, like catering? As soon as I asked, I realised it was a silly question; there are no corridors in the Isle of Man's Victorian coaches. Even so, a buffet car perhaps?

He explained there were special coaches which could be hired for hospitality jaunts, but the real problem was the track – and when I travelled on it myself, I realised what he meant. Any juggling you may have done on British Rail with a cup of coffee or a bowl of soup would be nothing compared with the acrobatics required on the Isle of Man Railway.

'The track is our biggest problem for the future. A

lot of trackwork needs to be done, and it's just a case of ploughing on with it. It's already improved over the last ten years, but an enormous backlog of under-investment has to be caught up with.

But I've no doubt that in time, if we have the continued support of the Manx government, we'll achieve it.'

That continued support is the cornerstone of the steam railway's future. Of the million-and-a-half pounds allocated to the three railways, it gets about £600,000. To make up for the lack of catering on the trains, pleasant new restaurants have been included in the restoration of the station buildings at Douglas and Port Erin. Robert Smith's policy is to deal with each station in turn, rather than spread his resources too thinly. Port Erin's turn came first. In 1990 the wooden panelling inside the station was restored and the decorative bargeboards on the roof replaced, all by the railway's own staff. On chilly days – even when I was there in mid-August – coal fires burn in the two big waiting-rooms. The stationmaster, Bob Western, makes sure there's a good blaze.

'Some of the children who come here have never seen a coal fire before, just as they've never seen a steam engine. I have to keep explaining to them that it's not a gas fire underneath.'

The locals were duly impressed by all this restoration work, and items began to emerge from lofts and garden sheds which had been 'rescued' years before when the line looked like closing. The station is well equipped with old bits of railway equipment, and vintage posters, and mirrors advertising long-forgotten patent medicines. It is now also displaying a Railway Heritage award.

In 1991 it was Douglas's turn. The old clock tower, on the point of collapse, was restored, and the top of it given a coat of gold leaf to match the domes and pinnacles over the station entrance. The century-old booking hall has a new wooden floor which looks more original than the original, even the 'No Waiting' signs in the forecourt have been painted in period style, and the plaques on the gates have been

repainted with the company's insignia.

There are hanging baskets in the forecourt and on the platform – but Robert Smith hopes it won't go any further. 'To use a horrible word, it's important we don't over-chintzify the railway. You can get carried away and make it over-pretty, so it loses its original character; that is something we are very conscious of.'

I can see his point. There is no great harm in a hanging basket or two, but the atmosphere of the Isle of Man Railway is so genuinely Victorian that it would be a pity to spoil it with fancy modern frills. So while the toilets and catering facilities are fully up-to-date, the seats in the trains are not too padded, and the old-fashioned windows and big brass doorhandles still have to be grappled with, and at some stops it is quite a long drop to ground level. This is the way our great-grandparents travelled, and Robert Smith is keeping it that way.

Passengers revel in the height of luxury, however, compared with the spartan conditions of the footplate.

The booking office at Port Erin Station.

Opposite: *No. 4, 'Loch', steaming past Ballybeg Halt.*

I was advised to get on board at Castletown, some ten miles outside Douglas, because by that time they would have used up some of the coal and there'd be more room in the cab. As it turned out, there was still a fair amount of coal about, and I had to perch on the edge of the footplate for much of the trip, but while I was waiting it did give me a chance to visit the stationmaster's office at Castletown, a marvellous little Victorian cameo, with two old armchairs drawn up to the coal fire, an old stand-up desk for issuing tickets, a battered iron kettle for brewing up tea, and some even more battered frying-pans on the wall for goodness knows what. Castletown is the next station on the list for restoration, to make it a more fitting arrival point for the most attractive little town on the island, but I hope they are not tampering with the stationmaster's office, no matter how old the armchairs or how battered the utensils. If its original occupant ever returned, he would feel perfectly at home.

And so would the original driver and fireman of *Hutchinson*, named after some long-forgotten company official and at 83 years of age one of the younger engines working on the line. *Hutchinson* has had a new boiler and larger tank, but the cab is just as cramped and it rocks just as much. Even so, the ride was well worthwhile, to see the old warrior in action and to meet its driver, Jack Petri.

Jack is an Italian Rhodesian who emigrated to Africa when he was eighteen and spent the next twenty-seven years on Rhodesian Railways; he was driving one of the enormous Garratt engines when Rhodesia became Zimbabwe. He discovered life was not too comfortable under the new regime, particularly when people took potshots at his engine. In 1983 he was ready to go back to Italy, but his wife came from the Isle of Man and she persuaded him to go there instead.

'Then I saw these little engines, just like toys after the Garratts I'd been driving, and I fell for them completely. I said I must get a job driving one of those, and I pestered the railway until they gave me a job as a fireman. I still fire sometimes to the senior drivers, but

Left: *No. 11, 'Maitland', built in 1905, in its Indian red livery formerly used by the Isle of Man Railway Company from the 1940's to 1966.*

Below: *Port Erin-bound train pulled by No. 4, 'Loch'.*

most of the time I'm driving.' He patted his 'toy' engine affectionately.

Like most of the staff on the railway, Jack turns his hand to other jobs too. His fireman on that run, Charlie Watson, was actually an apprentice joiner, and one stationmaster I met is also a driver, a fireman, a guard and a booking office clerk, and in the winter he works on the permanent way. Even the operations superintendent, Graham Warhurst, who has been part of the management since it was a private company, still stands in as a driver if need be. Robert Smith would rather like to; he has driven the buses and the electric trams, but it takes three years as a fireman before qualifying to drive a steam loco. 'You've got to know exactly what you're doing when you're driving one of those things, so they haven't let me loose on them yet.'

No other volunteers are let loose on them either. In fact, there are no volunteers working on the railway. That isn't deliberate policy, it is just because steam enthusiasts on the mainland are more likely to volunteer for the Ffestiniog or the Talyllyn than go to the expense and trouble of crossing to the Isle of Man. The local supporters' groups produce excellent magazines and give strong moral support – they are particularly vociferous if there is any hint of a closure – but their physical efforts have been concentrated on restoring a separate little line at Groundle Glen, just below the famous Great Wheel at Laxey.

Robert Smith does not rule out the possibility of volunteer helpers in the future. It would interest more people in the railway, as well as reducing costs – and in spite of that handsome subsidy, he still has to think about costs.

'Fortunately the House of Keys takes the view that the railway is an asset to be cherished, like the castles and the museums, and it demonstrates its support in this tangible form. But naturally it doesn't want to see its contribution increasing all the time. There are other things to spend money on. The government is conscious of that and so am I, so I don't want the deficit to run through the roof.'

He hopes to build up the private hire side, investigate the souvenir business – surprisingly there are no souvenir shops on any of the stations – and above all improve the quality of the product, and thus justify increased fares. 'As it is, I don't think you could travel fifteen miles on any other preserved railway in Britain for only £4.75 return; that's pretty reasonable. But I think people are prepared to pay more for a better quality product.'

That is a refreshingly forward-looking approach on an island which on the whole prefers to look back, whether it concerns using the birch, or the law on homosexuality, or the fairies who live by the Fairy Bridge, Manxmen may not seem too enlightened on the first two subjects, but I am sure that they have got it right about the fairies. Each time I visit the island I am careful to follow the tradition of saying hallo to them as I cross that bridge, lest I incur their wrath, and this time I was particularly wise to do so.

When we arrived in Douglas my wife discovered that her wallet was missing. She was convinced that she had it when we left home, and I had unpleasant visions of her credit cards being used on a spending spree at the airport. As a long shot we phoned our neighbours to check if she had left the wallet in another bag – and miraculously, unbelievably, it was there.

On our journey back to the airport at the end of our visit, it did not surprise me at all that our driver, a retired Manx railwayman who had lived on the island all his life, interrupted a quite normal conversation as we crossed the bridge to say hallo to the fairies. I didn't just say hallo; I said a grateful thank-you.

And I am sure that Robert Smith, the most fortunate man I've met in the world of little trains, in the job which must be every railway enthusiast's dream, keeps on the right side of the fairies too...

Leighton Buzzard
Railway

THE scene is a modern red-brick housing estate on the outskirts of Leighton Buzzard. Its centre-piece is an equally modern red-brick pub, unconvincingly named the Clay Pipe. It is lunchtime on a sunny Sunday in August. Light traffic moves smoothly along the main road through the estate, a handful of drinkers outside the pub watch it go by. A typically English suburban Sunday...

Enter, stage left, from between the houses a little way up the road, two men in blue overalls and shiny black caps, carrying red flags. They station themselves in the middle of the road, flags held aloft, and the traffic comes to a halt.

Offstage, the sound of an engine whistle, and onto the main road between two front gardens comes an elderly steam locomotive, black smoke pouring out of its funnel-shaped chimney, looking as if it has just emerged from a West African rubber plantation. It steams majestically across the road and into the maze of red-brick semis on the other side. Behind it are half-a-dozen red-painted wooden carriages, some open-sided, some with windows, all of them looking more suited to the turn of the century than 1990s suburbia.

The train stops, once it is clear of the road, for the flagmen to climb back on board, then it disappears among the back gardens. The traffic flows again, the sun still shines, the drinkers still drink – and if you had never seen it before, you might think it has all been a bizarre hallucination.

Well, the beer at the Clay Pipe is good, but not that good. The train was the 12.30 from Pages Park Station to the Stonehenge Works, and that unlikely engine was *Elf*, which really did originate from a Cameroon

Racing against 'Elf' on the outskirts of Leighton Buzzard.

133

Leighton Buzzard Light Railway

Page's Park Station, Billington Road, Leighton Buzzard, Beds, LU7 8TN. Tel. (0525) 373888

Route: Page's Park – Stonehenge Works
Distance: 2.75 miles
Gauge: 1 ft 11½ in
Service: Suns, B/H end March – beginning Oct, Wed/Th in August.

During the First World War sandpits were opened south of Leighton Buzzard, to make good the supply of sand which had previously come from Belgium. A narrow-gauge line was built to carry it, and this developed into a substantial system, worked at first by steam but later by diesel. When, in 1967, it seemed likely that the sandpits would close (as indeed they did in 1969), a Society was formed to prevent closure of the line, and on 3 March 1968 it ran its first passenger train – diesel-hauled – thereafter using the line regularly at weekends. The first steam engine, which arrived in June that year, was *Chaloner,* built in Wales in 1877, but since then a number of locomotives have found their way to the line from a number of different countries. An early task was the improvement of Page's Park station, the line's headquarters, and the building/acquisition of rolling stock. Since those early days the line has been extended to its present terminus, a brickworks called Stonehenge where many items of the railway's historic collection are now housed. It is also planned to set up a Museum focussing on the history of the local sand industry, without which, of course, the line would not exist.

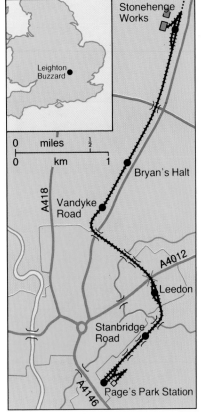

Below: *'Elf', steaming through a Leighton Buzzard housing estate.*

rubber plantation, but for the last twenty years has operated on the Leighton Buzzard Narrow-Gauge Railway, the only working wood-fired locomotive in the country.

Elf is one of many surprises, and many unique features, of an altogether surprising and unique little railway. I have often driven through Leighton Buzzard – or rather, round it, because the old town is now virtually stockaded behind supermarkets and car parks – but I had never associated it with the Little Trains of Britain, nor indeed regarded it as a tourist town. It does have an historic market cross, and there is a nice touch of whimsy about the almshouses, where according to tradition the founder's will is read aloud at Rogationtide, while a choirboy stands on his head. I rather hoped that the reason for the choirboy's curious gyration was to confuse some legendary buzzard associated with the town, but alas, there is no ornithological significance attached to Leighton Buzzard. The name came from a canon of Lincoln Cathedral called Theodore de Busna, who had the town in his pastoral care. Busna became corrupted (the name, not the canon) and finished up as Buzzard.

So there are no open moors around the town where these birds used to roam, just sand quarries, which are less scenic but a lot more profitable. Sand was Leighton Buzzard's main industry, and the quarries its main employers; it was because of all this sand that the Leighton Buzzard Light Railway was built in 1919, to become in later years one of Bedfordshire's most popular tourist attractions.

During the first World War the sand was being transported in lorries, which did no good at all to the local roads. The government kept them repaired as part of the war effort until 1919, then told the quarries it was up to them. The owners did some quick sums and decided it would be cheaper to build a railway instead – so long as costs were kept to a minimum. So they did – and they were. The result was three-and-a-half miles of two-foot gauge track which was thrown

Right: *Visiting 'Elidir' in Page's Park Station.*

together in just two months, for the modest figure of £12,030 13s 8d.

To do it, the contractor used much lighter rails than were specified, no effort was made to reduce the gradients, and corners were cut – quite literally – by bending straight rails into rough curves. It turned out to be arguably the worst stretch of railway line in the country.

This was the so-called 'main line' which ran past the quarries to the London and North Western Railway at Leighton Buzzard. Branch lines, a few hundred yards long, connected with each quarry along the route, and to haul the tipper waggons to the railhead, two steam locomotives were retrieved from the battlefields of France. They may have done well on the battlefields, but they were no match for this quite awful 'main line'. After two years of constant derailments, with extra irritations like the time taken to replenish the water tanks, and the high-quality sand being discoloured by soot, it was decided to replace them with powerful little petrol-driven engines, which held the rails better, wasted less time, and caused less dirt. Years ahead of the main railway network, the Leighton Buzzard Light Railway came to rely entirely on internal combustion.

Half a century later the story came full circle. The owners of the quarries and other industries which had grown up alongside the 'main line' started putting their freight traffic back on the roads, no doubt rejoicing that it was now the taxpayer who footed the bills. The little railway was needed less and less, and looked like falling into complete disuse. It was saved by voluntary effort – and the return of steam.

The way this revival came about was quite different from most railway preservation societies. This was not a group of enthusiasts appalled by the prospect of an historic line being lost for ever; it was largely a sheer fluke. The two people mainly responsible, Brian

Left: 'Elf', *the only wood-burning locomotive in Britain.*

Right: 'Chaloner', *built in 1877, pilots visiting loco 'Peter Pan'.*

Harris and Laurie Brooks, originally intended to build their own railway in Watford, and the only reason they came to Leighton Buzzard in 1967 was to pick up secondhand rails and equipment. They were quite astonished to find the line was still in use. So the bad news was, they could hardly rip up the rails while the sand waggons were still running on them, albeit spasmodically. The good news was that the quarry which owned the line was quite happy to let them use it at weekends, when the waggons were not working.

There were other unusual aspects of this rescue operation. In most cases the big attraction of preserving a narrow-gauge railway was its steam locomotives; Leighton Buzzard however was now operated entirely with Simplex diesel engines, direct descendants of the petrol-driven ones which took over from the steam locos in its early days. And there were of course no facilities for carrying people; a sand tipper truck is not exactly designed for passenger comfort.

On top of all this, Messrs Harris and Brooks and the other early participants really wanted to create an American format for their railway. They talked about depots instead of stations, engineers instead of drivers, and they chose to call themselves the Iron Horse Preservation Society. It is difficult to imagine anything less like the traditional American loco, with its cowcatcher and clanging bell, than the diminutive diesel 'iron horses' of Leighton Buzzard. Even when steam was brought back and passengers carriages were introduced, it was hard to detect any trans-Atlantic flavour.

Wisely, the members gave up their American dream and after two years they renamed themselves the Leighton Buzzard Narrow-Gauge Railway Society. But its origins were not entirely forgotten. With a nice touch of tongue-in-cheek, the Society's rulebook still contains as one of its objects, 'to encourage the study of environmental ferro-equinology...'

Sorting out the society's name was a very minor problem compared with what faced them out there on the decrepit 'main line'. The first job was to find something to run on it when it was available at weekends,

The all-clear given for the train leaving Page's Park Station.

A meal break, Page's Park Station.

Opposite: *'Elf' passes through open countryside on its return trip to Page's Park Station.*

something preferably capable of carrying passengers. They got hold of four old Simplex diesels from a sand quarry at St. Alban's, and extracted enough usable parts out of them to construct one serviceable engine. It was nicknamed, for reasons which soon became obvious, Smoky. Some open waggons were acquired and on March 3rd, 1968, the Society was ready to run the first passenger train in the history of the Leighton Buzzard Railway.

But there was a snag. The work on the Simplex engines had been carried out in a near-derelict shed on the far side of the road from where the 'main line' now ended at Page's Park. There was nothing new about crossing roads – the 'main line' has half-a-dozen level crossings along its route – but in this case there was no level crossing, just a road, and a busy main road at that, linking Leighton Buzzard with Hemel Hempstead.

Showing the talent for improvisation which has been a hallmark of the Society throughout its history, a length of portable track was acquired to span the road. The police agreed to hold up the traffic, and to the astonishment of the waiting motorists the reconstructed Simplex engine was pushed manually across the tarmac, a length of track at a time.

Safely on the other side, it was attached to the open waggons and the first intrepid passengers ever to ride on the 'main line' climbed aboard. There were no seats, so they stood shoulder to shoulder throughout the journey – 'like vertical sardines', as one eye-witness described it. Happily the seven-mile round trip was completed without the loss of a single passenger, and a new era in Leighton Buzzard's railway history had begun.

After celebrating this inaugural run, the founding members moved on to the next stage. They wanted passenger coaches, and they wanted steam. The coaches were created by fitting primitive wooden seats onto the flat waggons; steam arrived in the form of a most extraordinary old engine called *Chaloner*, known affectionately as the Galloping Tea Urn. Its central feature is a vertical boiler, with the firebox

underneath and a chimney on top. There is an eighty-gallon water tank at the front, and a coal bunker (where the driver sits) at the rear. The whole ensemble gives the impression of being put together by students in an engineering lab, as a practical joke.

Actually it was no joke – and it worked. It worked first of all in the North Wales slate quarries as far back as 1877; it worked on the 'main line' when the Society acquired it in 1968; and on special occasions it still works today.

Like a number of the engines which have been used at Leighton Buzzard it was originally bought by an individual member, in this case Alfred Fisher, later chairman of the Society. He gives a splendid description of its performance at the occasion of the official opening, which was scheduled for June 23rd, 1968, the day of the Town Carnival – 'it being decided by someone of supreme but misguided confidence that the inaugural train should carry the Carnival Queen and her retinue. However, during the final test *Chaloner* crossed the Hockliffe Road rather rapidly after stalling at the first attempt, dropped both fire and firebars in the middle of the A.4012, and de-railed once safely across.'

The Galloping Tea Urn, now only limping, returned to Pages Park with what steam pressures were left, and a Simplex was used for the run instead. It made the outward trip successfully hauling three waggonloads of passengers, but it returned, alas, with only two, since it lacked the power to pull all three up the gradients. Whereupon the Tea Urn came back into its own.

'*Chaloner*, now with fire up in its belly and 50 psi on the clock, was despatched posthaste to bring back the stray coach,' recalls Mr Fisher. 'This it triumphantly did, thus forming the first steam passenger train in the line's history...'

After this inauspicious launch, things could only get better. Another steam engine arrived, *Pixie*, a comparative youngster of more orthodox design, built in 1922. Two of the passenger waggons were provided with roofs as well as seats, and could reasonably be

called coaches. A brake van, essential on the steep gradients, was constructed by stripping the engine out of a redundant diesel and fitting it with a carriage body.

A platform was built at Pages Park, and an empty shell of a building was converted into a booking hall and ticket office, with a bookshop and buffet. The Council said it had no planning permission and ordered the building to be demolished. Then it took a second look and said don't bother, it'll fall down anyway in a year. It stands there still.

Gradually the Society took over the entire running of the railway, and the last sand train came down to Pages Park in 1977. However, the far end of the 'main line' was covered over and used by lorries serving the remaining quarry, so passenger trains have to turn round after two-and-three-quarter miles at what used to be Stonehenge Brickworks. Hence the confusing announcement at Pages Park: 'All aboard for Stonehenge...'

There was a hiccup in the steady progress of the

Steam day with No. 3, 'Rishra', No. 4, 'Doll', in the background and visiting loco 'Peter Pan' in the foreground.

Opposite: *The Stonehenge Works-bound train waits for the Page's Park train to pass on the Leedon loop.*

Society when the last stretch of track to Stonehenge deteriorated so badly that it became unusable. It took four years, ten thousand pounds – of which the members raised half – and a lot of help from the County Council and the Youth Opportunities Programme to reconstruct it, but in 1982 there was a triumphant 'Return to Stonehenge', and since then it has been comparatively smooth running, not only on that section of line but for the development of the railway.

I experienced the delights of the 'main line' from the footplate of *Elf*, I was provided with the full trappings of blue overalls and shiny black cap, and I soon wished I had goggles too; the windows of *Elf* have been taken out to make the cab cooler, but it makes it smokier and sootier too. Old railway sleepers do not make the cleanest fuel...

We were despatched from Pages Park by Colin Bassett, whose successful slimming campaign had earned him the title of the Thin Controller. Our train crew of five – driver, fireman, guard and two flagmen

'Rishra' and 'Peter Pan' pulling the Stonehenge Works-bound train.

– included Ian Gaylor, one of the earliest members, who had recently returned to the Society. Ian had been a fully qualified driver, but after his absence he was happy to start again at the bottom as a flagman and cleaner. From my position on the footplate I could understand why re-training was necessary; it takes a lot of regular practice to negotiate the steep gradients and sharp bends, and I gather the drivers of visiting engines can find the 'main line' very disconcerting. Marley's Bank, for instance, is a gradient of one in 25 with a sharp bend at the bottom. To an unsuspecting driver, arriving at the top of the bank can seem like going over the top of a Big Dipper. Wisely, every visiting engine crew is accompanied by a local member.

There is also a great deal of starting and stopping because of all the level crossings along the route. The flagmen have enlivened this rather tedious procedure by devising a highly unofficial points system, involving the type of vehicles they hold up. A police car, I understand, counts three points; if its blue light is flashing, it counts five. One train scored nine points for a funeral procession, and I think the record was held at one stage by a flagman who managed to stop the same lorry three times, at three different crossings.

Because of all these stops, and the bends and gradients, *Elf* averages little more than five miles an hour, but there is, after all, no hurry. As the track often runs alongside roads and footpaths we had some interesting competition from joggers, cyclists and small children. The cyclists won easily, and one jogger stayed ahead of us for a mile or more – but we did beat a six-year-old on a trike...

Apart from this extra entertainment, a casual visitor who has been to other narrow-gauge railways might find the pattern at Leighton Buzzard familiar, on the surface at least, the Victorian-style open carriages and the antique engines, and a few miles of rather bumpy track to nowhere in particular. Even its slogan, 'England's Friendly Little Line', is not just applicable to Leighton Buzzard; I have yet to find a little line that isn't. But it does have some special features which make it quite different from any other I have seen.

To begin with, there are its incongruous surroundings, epitomised by that strange vision manifested to the lunchtime drinkers outside the Clay Pipe. When the railway was taken over, it ran mainly through open country, except for the quarries and later the brickworks and other industries it served. Then in the 1970s a rash of new houses appeared around Leighton Buzzard. The population soared from fewer than twenty thousand to more than thirty-four thousand – and a great many of the newcomers came to live in the housing estates alongside the line.

This has presented the railway with some new problems, quite apart from losing much of its rural scenery. The children living by the track, for instance, are inclined to put the odd stone on the rails or even shy one at the engine, though the drivers and guards know which are the problem areas and have ways of coping. On the other hand the residents can have their problems too. Lines of washing do not always improve after a woodburning engine has passed by, and I suspect that many a Sunday afternoon snooze must have been interrupted by *Elf*'s whistle.

The railway volunteers do not feel too guilty about this. They point out gently that they were there before the houses, and the occupants must have known what to expect when they moved in. But they do their best to keep on good terms. At one of the crossings, for example, where back gardens run alongside the line, the train always pulls up well short of them. It means a long run up the line for the flagmen to reach the crossing, but it also means a more peaceful afternoon for the people who live there.

It is not housing all the way. Pages Park Station is in fact on the edge of a public park, which provides a green and leafy backdrop to the platform – though it does lead the unbriefed visitor to expect that the railway is just one of those miniature jobs that are set up inside parks. On the opposite side of the station is a small working sand quarry, a reminder of the railway's original raison d'etre, though the sand is taken away in lorries now.

There are more open spaces before the estates begin, and beyond them, for the last mile to Stonehenge, it is just open fields – or the open range, as the Iron Horse Society would have called it. But it is the anachronism of finding vintage trains steaming through modern housing estates which sticks in my mind. It is rather like finding the *Rocket* operating on the Piccadilly Line between Uxbridge and Rayners Lane.

Once you get to the end of the run from Pages Park and into the workshops at Stonehenge, another difference becomes apparent. This is very much a do-it-yourself railway. It could well use the motto of the Round Table movement: 'Adopt, Adapt, Improve'. The workshops themselves were originally the stables of the Stonehenge brickworks, housing the horses which hauled the brick trucks before the railway was there. They were built by POWs during the first World War, and they left an ingenious gesture of defiance in the brickwork. They laid the stones in one wall in the shape of a phallic symbol...

Fifty-odd years later the railway volunteers con-

'Chaloner' *heading* 'Peter Pan' *over one of the many level crossings on the Leighton Buzzard line.*

verted the ground floor into repair shops and the loft into a carpenter's shop and signals store. Virtually everything on the railway, apart from the actual engines, has been made in these buildings, and even some of the engines have been entirely rebuilt. The carriages may look Victorian, but with one exception they were all built by Society members. The chassis and bogies had to be imported, but when I was there they were working on Carriage 12, which has a home-made chassis and bogies as well as homemade bodywork and fittings. Even the machinery to build the carriage was made or adapted in the workshop; the gantry, for example, used to be a metal footbridge from further down the track.

Carriage 12 was being supervised by David Barrow, who joined the Society when he was sixteen and has spent more than half his life as a volunteer. Out in the real world he works for the Inland Revenue, but in the 'Doll's House' – named after an engine which it used to house – he is the foreman-carpenter. There has been some outside help in manpower and money. Four or five lads worked there under a Manpower Services scheme, and because carriage 12 is designed to take wheelchairs the local Lions donated £2500, enough to have the carriage doors copied from a prototype which David made. But in the main this is genuine DIY, and as a result it all takes a little time. As David told me with obvious regret: 'Other jobs crop up in the workshops and I can only spend about half my railway time on Number 12. It can be frustrating when all you want to do is push on with it.' So a project like this can last years – but he was determined to get the new carriage onto the track in the Society's jubilee year, 1992.

At Leighton Buzzard they are not only into DIY but also OIY – Own It Yourself. Only one of the six engines is actually owned by the Society as a whole; the others belong to individual members or are on permanent loan, For instance *Rishra*, a 1921 engine which spent most of its working life at a pumping station near Calcutta, was discovered by Mike Satow while he was working in India. It was lying derelict with its cab in the bushes and a clothesline tied to its chimney. He had it shipped home via Leighton Buzzard in two packing cases in the early days of the Society, and he liked the set-up there so much that, although he lives in Newcastle, he keeps *Rishra* there and in due course became the Society's president.

This OIY system is not confined to steam engines. There is a remarkable assortment of diesels at Leighton Buzzard, from *The Bedstead*, which has a metal canopy like a fourposter, to an elegant model with semi-automatic transmission called *Falcon*, owned by the present chairman, Tony Tomkins. Tony is a frequent visitor to Saudi Arabia, and the diesel's name is also written on the engine in Arabic lettering. It is therefore known disrepectfully as *Squiggle*.

Perhaps the most enthusiastic exponent of OIY is Rod Dingwall, who actually sold his car so he could buy more rolling-stock. His current list comprises two Simplex diesels, one coach and seventeen waggons – 'and one day I hope to have a steam engine'. He lives in a house alongside the line, and although he is in London each morning in time to start at a publishing firm at 8.30, and only gets home about twelve hours later, every other waking moment, it seems, is spent on the railway.

Officially Rod is the Society's fundraiser, but I gather every member provides funds, or materials, or some form of expertise. They range from Derek Trevilion, the guard on the train I travelled on, who is a structural engineer and thus invaluable when awkward inclines need to be regraded, to Chris Coombes, who works in the diesel repair shop. He is normally in the waste disposal business, so the railway gets a steady supply of paint, sealing compounds, glues...

The Society, in fact, has a simple recipe for success: never buy what you can get for nothing. And it has another maxim which becomes apparent as soon as you enter the workshops: never throw anything away.

Chris is known as Chris Number One, because there are several volunteers with the same name and he has been there the longest. He lives in Chelmsford and

Visiting loco 'Elidir'.

explain, with appropriate gestures. 'It means the valves go this way instead of that way. It was somebody's idea to get a very small combustion chamber in the cylinder head, to get more efficient combustion.'

'Of course', I said – and changed the subject. 'What are you working on now?'

Chris Number One gave it some thought. 'Well, I'm supposed to be doing a quick job of fitting airbrakes to a diesel to provide another spare loco. That was about Easter.' It was now August. 'Various things have conspired to make it take a little longer.'

It confirmed the impression I had got from David Barrow and his Carriage 12. Life would be a lot simpler in the workshops if they didn't have to keep the railway running.

I had assumed that repairing and maintaining diesel engines big enough to haul trains would need expert engineering knowledge, but Chris Number One made light of it. 'I picked it up as I went along, and I got some books on old diesel engines from second-hand bookshops which helped. You don't need to know much more than you do to overhaul a car engine, except the engine's bigger and stronger, of course. You just need bigger and stronger spanners.'

He went on talking about his diesels with obvious affection – in contrast to the average narrow-gauge enthusiast, for whom steam is all. Usually it is the younger generation which is more diesel-minded, but that doesn't apply at Leighton Buzzard. Alistair Chisholm, for instance, was only fifteen when I met him but he was looking forward to training as a fireman in three years' time. What's the attraction, I asked.

'Well, steam engines are totally different from anything that's around these days,' he explained. 'With diesels you just turn a key and it goes. With steam you've got three or four hours' preparation before you can do anything with it.'

A strange sort of attraction, I thought, but Nick Williams, who was with us, backed him up. Nick's devotion to steam is such that he spends two hours

works near the Dartford Tunnel, but he's been spending his spare time fifty miles away at Leighton Buzzard for the last twenty-odd years. He decided the steam side was too competitive – 'everyone wanted to do it' – so after a year he bought his first petrol engine and started restoring it. He's been devoted to petrol and diesel engines ever since, though they had to take second place when he became permanent way engineer for twelve years.

'Diesels are considered the poor relation, but I reckon they're more interesting. Just in our collection here we've got so many wierd and wonderful designs, different ideas people had for improving transmission for instance. There are some really wierd engines knocking about under all these bonnets. The wierdest one...' he paused for effect – '...has horizontal valves operated through angle cranks!'

I registered astonishment, but my ignorance of steam engines is matched only by my ignorance of diesels, and it obviously showed. Chris tried to most Sundays sawing up old sleepers to feed into *Elf's* firebox. 'Steam will always get you there and get you back,' he said fondly. 'Even if it's in trouble it still limps home. If a diesel packs up, then that's it.'

Alistair joined in again. 'If you treat steam engines right, they'll treat you right. Diesel is just a thing, a piece of machinery, but a steam engine has got personality..'

I left them agreeing with each other; it was a familiar routine. Diesels have their place at Leighton Buzzard, but steam is still holding its own.

Rod Dingwall led me up the line beyond the Stonehenge Works. There are only a few hundred yards of worn and overgrown track, and at present it is just used for storing surplus waggons, but one day they plan to open it up again, not just this stretch but right to the terminus of the original 'main line'. The track ended at a gate, and Rod showed me where the lorries drove over the rest of the trackbed, before turning off towards the quarry. One day, he told me, though he wasn't sure when, the lorries were due to be diverted off the trackbed onto a different route, and that would bring the line's completion a stage nearer.

We were walking towards the quarry now, and as we reached it Rod gave a shout of astonished delight. I was only looking at the vast crater ahead of us, the colour of the sand altering at different levels from white to light brown, to dark grey, making it look like an enormous decorated sugar-bowl; but Rod was looking at a newly-constructed track which led out of the quarry – and away from the old railway.

'They've done it!' he shouted. 'They've made a new track for the lorries. They won't be using the old trackbed any more.' He was exultant, and I had the rather exhilirating feeling that I was present at a little moment in railway history...

As we hurried back with the news he told me about their other plans. They had made a deal with the owner of the quarry next to Pages Park to put up a new station building, a two-storey affair with a members' bar and meeting room upstairs. He had some new ideas for special days like the annual Teddy Bears' Outing. They were restoring more engines, steam and diesel, and Carriage 12 would be able to take disabled passengers instead of putting them in the guard's van, and they'd have new workshops so the old stables at Stonehenge could be turned into a railway museum, and...

The list went on. If I heard it anywhere else I might have been sceptical, but at Leighton Buzzard it all seemed entirely feasible. In its first twenty-five years this enterprising little Society of only three hundred members has attracted over a quarter of a million passengers, it has relaid the track, built its own rolling-stock, accumulated an amazing collection of locomotives, produced the best-written quarterly magazine I have yet come across among the Little Trains, established itself firmly on the tourist map of the county – and is still panting for more.

'It's called 'planning for growth',' said Rod proudly.

It's also called enthusiasm – plus of course never buying what you can get for nothing, and never throwing anything away...

'Elf' *originally came from the Tiko Rubber Mill in the French Cameroons.*

Below: 'Chaloner' *built in 1877, the oldest loco on the line.*

Talyllyn Railway

By rights it should have been called the Abergynolwyn Railway, which is the village where the passenger line terminated, or even the Bryn Eglwys Railway, the name of the quarry which it served. It might even have been named after the valley which it runs through, the Nant Gwernol. Instead, for reasons which not even its official guide-book explains, the Talyllyn was named after a tiny village three miles away. It is only a handful of cottages and a couple of hotels alongside a pleasant lake, but its name has become internationally famous, thanks to the Talyllyn Railway Preservation Society, formed in 1950 and the first society of its kind in the world.

So why Talyllyn? When the railway celebrated its 125th birthday the anniversary guidebook failed to produce any explanation. 'Why the railway was called Talyllyn is not known,' it says firmly. 'There was never any intention to extend the railway to the lake.'

The Talyllyn Handbook, a more technical and detailed production, does not seem to discuss the question at all. Even the proprietor of the Minffordd Hotel at Talyllyn, a railway enthusiast who decorates the guest rooms with photographs of steam trains, and gave me J.I.C. Boyd's monumental history of the Talyllyn for bedtime reading, had no idea how it got its name. Since I was only there for two nights I did not get far enough into Mr Boyd to find out if he gave the answer, but happily all was revealed to me by an equally unimpeachable source, the general manager of the railway, David Woodhouse.

The answer is ridiculously simple. By one of those quirks of local government, the village of Aber-gynolwyn is actually in the parish of Talyllyn. The McConnel family, who had the railway built mainly to

No. 2, 'Dolgoch', approaching Abergynolwyn.

Talyllyn Railway

Wharf Station, Tywyn, Gwynedd, LL36 9EY.
Tel. (0654) 710472

Route: Tywyn (Wharf) – Nant Gwernol
Distance: 7.5 miles
Gauge: 2 ft 3 in
Service: Daily, Easter – beginning Nov, 26 Dec – 1 Jan;
Santa specials

Like the Ffestiniog Railway, the Talyllyn began as a line to serve slate quarries and to bring the product to the coast. The original plan here was that the railway should run to the port of Aberdovey, but this was modified to an interchange wharf beside the Cambrian Railways' line at Tywyn, where the present Wharf terminus now stands. Unlike the Ffestiniog however, passengers were carried from the line's opening in 1866. In 1946 the slate quarry closed, but the railway was kept going as a local service by its owner Sir Henry Haydn Jones, at his own expense. Little was done in the way of maintenance, but when closure became imminent after Sir Henry's death in 1950, a group of volunteers stepped in and established the world's first railway preservation scheme. The Preservation Society has run the line ever since, in 1976 opening to passengers a .75-mile extension from Abergynolwyn along the old mineral line to the foot of the first of the inclines which led to the quarry. There have been other developments too, new carriages and, in 1991, a new engine, but the two original locomotives and 4-wheeled coaches are lovingly preserved in traffic: thus is ensured that much of the original Victorian atmosphere is retained, as was the intention of those first volunteers.

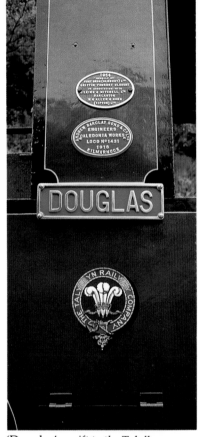

'Douglas', a gift to the Talyllyn Railway in 1953.

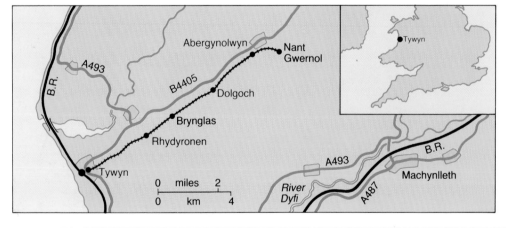

take slate from their quarry at Bryn Eglwys to the main line at Towyn, presumably had the privilege of naming it, as they were Manchester folk with no particular Welsh connections; maybe they thought that Talyllyn was marginally easier to pronounce than either Abergynolwyn or Bryn Eglwys. Certainly it proved more convenient when the line's first engine was named after the railway. *Abergynolwyn* would have been quite a handful to fit on the nameplate.

David Woodhouse not only knows the origin of the name, he knows just about everything there is to know about the Talyllyn Railway. When I met him he had just completed forty years' service with it, first as a volunteer, then as full-time traffic manager from 1966, finally as general manager from 1982. He has been involved in every stage of its restoration, ever since an imaginative and farsighted railway enthusiast called Tom Rolt called a meeting in his home city of Birmingham, to save the apparently doomed little railway.

Like others of its kind it had fallen on hard times. If it had not been for another great enthusiast, Henry Haydn Jones, it would have succumbed long before. He was a local landowner and businessman who took over the railway and the quarry when the McConnels wanted to close everything down in 1911, and thus saved the jobs of nearly all the working men in Abergynolwyn. He kept things going until 1946, when a disastrous series of rockfalls forced him to close the quarry. For years there had been very little money to spare for repairs and maintenance on the railway, and logically he should have closed that too, but to his great credit Sir Henry, as he now was, promised he would keep it going for as long as he lived.

That was the good news. The bad news was that, like the railway itself, Sir Henry was now over eighty. The long-term future of the Talyllyn did not look too rosy.

Nevertheless, Sir Henry and therefore the railway had another four years to go, and in that time he even

Right: *The sylvan setting of Rhydyronen Station.*

managed to have one of its original engines repaired, *Dolgoch*, probably at his own expense. The railway also survived nationalisation in 1948; the theory is that the government had no idea it was still functioning, because no returns had been made since before the first World War...

When Sir Henry died in 1950, however, the railway was in a state of 'advanced decrepitude', as one writer put it. Its time, it seemed, had come. Manifestly it was a hopeless financial investment; no businessman could regard it as a commercial proposition. Instead, Tom Rolt and his friends devised an entirely new concept, a railway operated by a preservation society, relying almost entirely on unpaid voluntary staff.

It is an idea which has been taken up to save many other narrow-gauge railways since, including Big Brother up the coast at Ffestiniog a few months later, but the Talyllyn claims to be the first in the field. The original Talyllyn Railway Company also had the distinction of being created by special Act of Parliament in 1865. So was the Ffestiniog, thirty-three years earlier, so the Talyllyn has to accept second place in that, but I suppose it could argue that it was still running when the preservation society took it over, whereas the Ffestiniog was out of action for five years. But on the other hand...

So the claims and counter-claims can go on. But the rivalry is friendly, and anyway there is something unique about every Little Train in Britain and all the Great Little Trains of Wales. Any student of English grammer can tell you that there are no degrees of uniqueness, so every little railway is as special as the next...

Being created by an Act of Parliament may sound very grand, but in fact the McConnel family did not seem too overawed at the time. Work actually started on the railway a year before the Act was passed. The first engines, *Talyllyn* and *Dolgoch*, were also ordered well before Parliament gave its approval. Maybe the McConnels had some inside knowledge about the

Left: *'Dolgoch' on an up train just outside Tywyn.*

way things were going in Whitehall; more likely they assumed nobody would notice what they were up to in their remote Welsh valley. The official handbook prefers not to commit itself:

'The railway was to all intents and purposes built without Parliamentary sanction, which was only obtained at a late stage and for reasons which are not yet clear.'

Whatever machinations went on behind it, the Act caused certain complications 85 years later when the preservation society took over. A new company had to be formed, Talyllyn Holdings Ltd, for the primary purpose of holding in trust the shares of the original company. But both companies have the same five directors; three of them, including the chairman, are appointed by the preservation society, the other two are members of the Hayden Jones family, Sir Henry's grandson and a cousin.

So in effect the society controls the railway, but in a rather roundabout fashion. As I understand it – and it takes some understanding – the members decide policy on operational matters, they tell the society council, the council tells the Board of Directors, and the Board of Directors tells the general manager. But very naturally the members like to take a hand themselves, and sometimes David Woodhouse can find himself, as he admits rather ruefully, the pig in the middle...

The Act of Parliament caused another complication. It only authorised the passenger railway to go as far as Abergynolwyn. The McConnels continued the track up the valley for another three-quarters of a mile to get within reach of their quarry at Bryn Eglwys, which was the main point of building the railway in the first place. This meant that from Towyn to Abergynolwyn it was a public passenger railway, but beyond Abergynolwyn it was designed as a private mineral railway, quite unsuited to passenger traffic. Even then it did not actually reach the quarry; the final phase was a steep incline from the track up to the quarry workings, and the slate trucks were lowered down to the track on ropes.

So when the preservation society took over, they could only run trains as far as Abergynolwyn – and even that was quite an effort. But that final three-quarters of a mile to the quarry, through the heavily-wooded gorge of the Nant Gwernol valley, was obviously the most dramatic and picturesque section of the line. If they could open that up as well, the Talyllyn's value as a tourist attraction would be vastly increased. It was a dream that took a quarter of a century to achieve, but they got there in the end.

Meanwhile there was quite enough work to be done on the track they had got. Veterans like David Woodhouse and the present chairman of the company, Peter Bold, who attended the original meeting at Birmingham, can recall hair-raising experiences from their early days as volunteers. David Woodhouse remembers being warned when working on the track that he could remove the turf from inside the rails, but on no account should he remove it from the outside until they were properly re-laid, because it was only

No. 6, 'Douglas', about to pull out of Wharf Station, Tywyn.

Below: *Two engine drivers from the Talyllyn Railway.*

No. 6, 'Douglas', taking on water at Dolgoch Falls Station.

Opposite: *Built in 1864, No. 1, 'Talyllyn', on Dolgoch Viaduct.*

the turf that was holding them to the right gauge.

'It was not unusual to be on a loco when the wheels hit one end of a rail joint, to see the other end of the rail go up and down again ahead of you. Derailments were not exactly infrequent in those days.'

Peter Bold is an engineer, but he worked on the track too, as well as firing the engines and working in the sheds. 'We just came up and asked what needed doing – and did it.' These days he has to spend a lot of time chairing meetings and attending committees, but he still gets into overalls and lends a hand when needed. After forty years the Talyllyn has not lost its original atmosphere, the spirit of pulling together that got the railway back on its feet in the 1950s, and made it possible to open the final section through the Nant Gwernol gorge in the 1970s.

Just the legal requirements for this proposed extension were daunting enough. It took years of negotiation to acquire the land and obtain an Order under the Light Railways Act to operate a public passenger service beyond Abergynolwyn. Then the real work began. In 1970, twenty years after he had called the meeting to form the society, Tom Rolt got things under way with a mighty blast – not on a trumpet or an engine whistle, but with explosives, the first of many blasting charges to clear thousands of tons of rock along the route.

David Woodhouse explained to me what was involved . 'We virtually had to build a new railway. In the earlier years we had lifted all the rail from that stretch which could be used elsewhere, and anyway the curves and clearances between the track and the rockface were not suitable for passenger trains. Luckily one of our volunteers was born and brought up in Cornish tin-mining, and he was a licensed shot-firer, so he thoroughly enjoyed himself.' David permitted himself a reminiscent smile. 'We only had one complaint from the village of Abergynolwyn, when they were showered with bits of rock one day...'

It took six years to complete the work. The Nant Gwernol section was formally opened by my former broadcasting colleague, the late Wynford Vaughan Thomas, on May 22nd 1976, and one of the original engines, *Dolgoch*, suitably flag-bedecked, hauled a special train from Abergynolwyn station to the new terminus of the railway, a little wooden hut and platform perched on the edge of the ravine.

It must have been a spectacular ride for the VIPs, and it still is today. First, the line clings to a ledge cut in the hillside overlooking the village, then there is a brief reminder of present-day transport as the line crosses a Forestry Commission road, before entering the trees again. On one side a waterfall cascades down the hillside, on the other is what's left of the old winding drum which, until 1947, lowered coal and stores down an incline to the village below – and hauled up the contents of the cesspits in return!

Then along another ledge cut in the rock-face, with the River Gwernol far below, and round a final sharp curve to Nant Gwernol station, on its narrow shelf above the ravine. Ahead the line peters out at the foot of the incline where the slate was lowered down from

the quarry. There is no way out there, and no road to continue the journey, just a few footpaths winding through the woods and up the valley. If ever a railway terminus epitomised the End of the Line, Nant Gwernol is it.

But it is not only the most isolated terminus I have visited, it is also the most picturesque – a striking contrast, if my friends up the coast will forgive me, to the bleak grey surroundings of Blaenau Ffestiniog. You may just like to stay on the platform and admire the view, while the engine runs round the train to take you back down again, or you may prefer to set off along the waymarked walks and explore the forest. If you are wise you will check the train times to make sure you are not marooned, but at a pinch you can always take the path back to Abergynolwyn.

The station at Abergynolwyn is rather more sophisticated than the one at Nant Gwernol – it was after all the terminus for many years – and all the trains wait there for half-an-hour on the way back down the valley, not only to give the walkers a chance to catch up, but to give passengers the chance to visit the souvenir shop and the refreshment room, and indeed the new toilets, built in 1990 with help from the Welsh Tourist Board and the Development Board for Rural Wales. They covered half the cost, the only kind of public grant the railway has received.

While we waited on the station I had a chat with the signalman, Lawrence Garvey from Birmingham, a volunteer for twenty-two years and one of the workers on the Nant Gwernol extension. He and his wife Jane both spend their holidays working on the Talyllyn. At present their five-year-old twins are looked after by their grandparents – 'but if they don't volunteer too in due course, they'll be in trouble!'

He told me that Jane was on duty at a passing loop at Quarry Siding, further down the line. It struck me that even during the peak season there are only five trains each way on the Talyllyn, and while Lawrence had the station staff to chat to, Jane at Quarry Siding was stuck in the middle of nowhere; the quarry is now completely overgrown and the line is well away from

The cab of No. 2, 'Dolgoch'.

Rest stop, Rhydyronen Station.

Opposite: *'Dolgoch' with an up train on its approach to Quarry Siding Halt. Here there is a passing loop and a siding which formerly served a shale quarry.*

any road. What on earth possesses people, I wondered, to spend their holidays like this?

Lawrence couldn't help me. 'You can ask anybody who's been a volunteer for ten, or fifteen, or twenty-two years, and I don't think any of us will be able to explain it to you. It's almost like a drug – you need to have a regular "fix"!'

Later, back on the train, I made a point of waving to Jane as we went through Quarry Siding, and she waved cheerfully back from the tiny little cabin where she was spending her day. She handed over the single-line token for the next section of track, exchanged a word with the driver and guard, and then we were on our way again and she was left there, alone, until the next train passed through, an hour or so later. Wonderfully peaceful, marvellous views, but even so, there must be more too it than that. Lawrence had given me half an answer; it was not Jane, but another woman volunteer, who gave me the rest of it. But that was to come later, at the end of the journey. There was much to see first...

Dolgoch Falls Station is in a setting nearly as spectacular as Nant Gwernol. The falls are just beside it in a wooded ravine, and the railway crosses it on a three-arched viaduct, fifty feet high. It was difficult to decide which view was the more impressive, looking up at the train from the ravine or down into the ravine from the train. The viaduct was the most expensive item in building the line, all of £3000 in 1865, but apart from an extensive overhaul twenty-odd years ago and a regular inspection it has not cost much since. The mishap on the Welshpool & Llanfair, when a river bridge was badly damaged by floodwaters, has happily not been repeated on the Talyllyn.

Beyond Dolgoch the line runs down into open country, through a deep cut which was so badly drained in the early days that the volunteers called it Tadpole Cutting. Cader Idris, second highest mountain in Wales, dominates the countryside here, but for the rest of the run, through the little stations of Brynglas and Rhydyronen (which I thought must be Welsh for Rhododendron, but it turns out to mean, strangely, Ashford), it is pastoral scenery populated mainly by sheep and cattle. In these peaceful surroundings we had our most dramatic moment: a large black cow appeared on the line ahead, and in spite of much whistle-blowing and waving of arms it refused to budge.

I gather such encounters are fortunately rare these days, though on one occasion the train had to contend with an entire flock of sheep, which took some time to disperse. In our case the little engine managed to outstare the cow, and it eventually trotted off down the track ahead of us, urged on by encouraging blasts on the whistle as we puffed along behind it. It found the gap in the fence it had escaped through, and the gap was duly noted. Adequate fencing is one of the problems on the Talyllyn. The traditional method is to plant long slivers of slate in the ground, close enough together to stop livestock getting through, but some of the animals seem to have got the hang of this, and more sophisticated fencing is being introduced.

The fields gave way to an industrial estate on one side and an electricity sub-station on the other. We were leaving the delights and excitement of the Snowdonia National Park for the rather less scenic environs of Tywyn (the spelling is now de-Anglicised). The line ends at Tywyn Wharf, where the slate used to be transferred to the main line. The preservation society has transformed it into a passenger terminus which is now a lot busier during the summer months than the main line station itself. In fact, tickets for British Rail are sold at the Talyllyn station, a curious reversal of roles and a useful little earner for the society.

This extra income goes towards repairing and maintaining and developing the Talyllyn. So do the profits from the souvenir shops and refreshment rooms, and the contract engineering work. David Woodhouse reckons to cover his direct operating costs from fares, but that's only because nearly all the operational work is done by volunteers. The society has three thousand members and about a tenth of them actively help on the railway; that seems to be the average percentage among railway preservation societies. There are just fourteen full-time permanent staff, most of them in the offices or the workshops. Even so, as David explained, the Talyllyn has to attract plenty of passengers to survive, and it isn't easy.

'The problem is that we are a tourist attraction in a comparatively remote part of the country. We are not on a main through route, we're in a bit of a backwater really. So we have to work hard to attract the customers.'

Of all the descriptions that came to mind when I looked around Tywyn, 'backwater' was not one of them; the streets were packed with holidaymakers. That was thanks to a Victorian salt magnate from Droitwich, John Corbett, who decided to acquire and develop the land between the town and the sea, back in its Towyn days. Until then it was owned by the Corbets of Moreton in Shropshire, whose interests lay in other directions. 'They were profligates who whored, gambled and drank away a fine inheritance,' wrote one blunt historian – and part of that inheritance was Towyn.

The new ownership must have been very beneficial to the Corbet Arms Hotel, which was no doubt happy to add another 't' to its name, and the Towyn this tavern was in became transformed. John Corbett built a road to link it with the sea, surrounded it with houses, created an esplanade on the sea-wall, and turned it into a mass-appeal holiday resort. When I enquired in the tourist office at Aberdovey, the fishing harbour down the coast, what I should see in Tywyn, the lady paused for a moment, then said carefully, 'You'll see a lot of people.' Actually there are a lot of people in Aberdovey too in the holiday season, but even when it is crowded it is still attractive. When Tywyn is crowded it is still – Tywyn.

But surely, I said to David, with so many people around there must be plenty of passengers for the Talyllyn. Like the lady in the tourist office he paused before replying. 'Tywyn is very much a caravan place,'

Right: 'Talyllyn', *makes its way down to Quarry Sidings.*

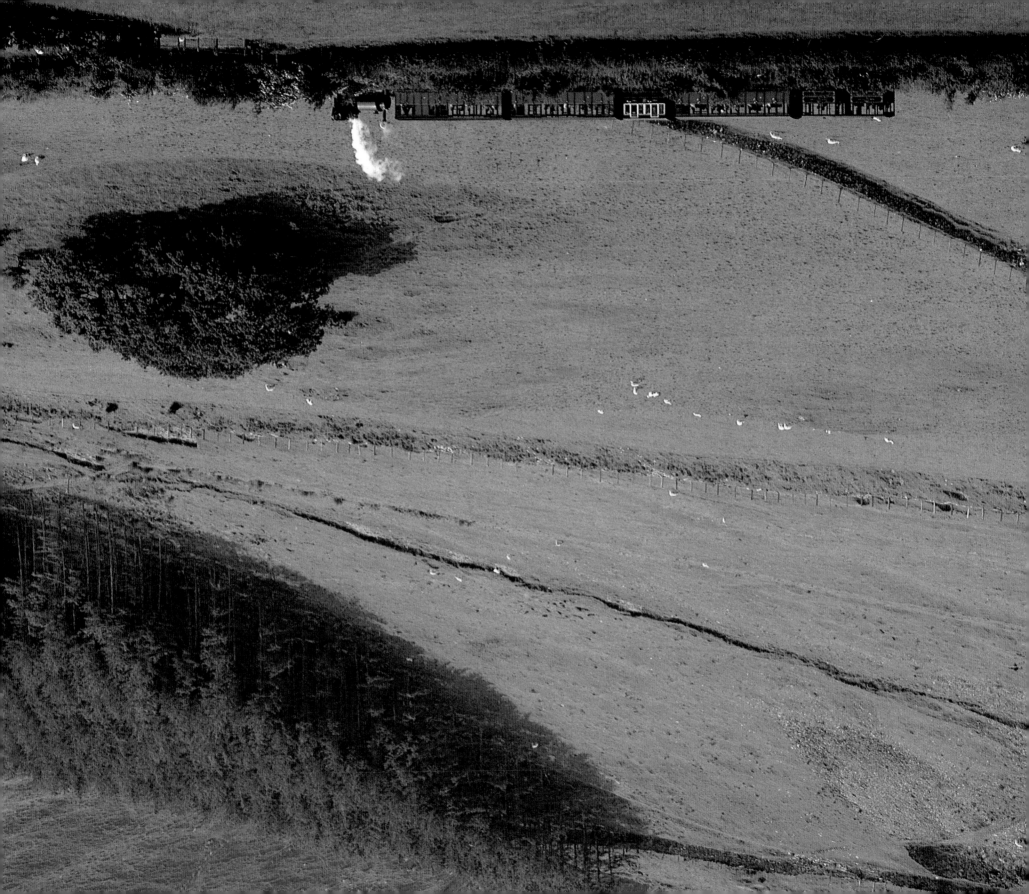

he said, just as carefully. 'The caravans are mostly owned by families who come every year. They might visit the railway the first year, but they wouldn't come again for the next two or three. No, most of our customers come from further afield.'

How about the locals, I asked, any support from them? There was another of those pauses. 'I think it's fair to say that the railway does a lot more for the town than the town does for us. But we do have half-a-dozen volunteers who live locally. They've retired and moved here just to work on the railway – from London, the south of England, all over. We rely on them a lot, especially early and late in the season.'

He relaxed a little. 'Some of them must regret they came here. Instead of retirement they found themselves working seven days a week!'

I met one or two of them, and of course they had no regrets. The Talyllyn attracts great devotion from a wide assortment of volunteers from far-flung corners of Britain. I discovered one who came from Thurso in the far north of Scotland, and you can't fling much further than that. And I even met a fireman called Timson. But I had yet to meet a rather special type of volunteer whom I had heard about on other railways but never actually encountered. I suppose the correct term would be female fire-persons; I prefer to call them lady firemen.

I had actually waved to one, at the Quarry Siding, because when Jane Garvey isn't operating the points at lonely loops she is shovelling coal on a footplate. But there was not exactly time for a chat during the brief stop at the loop, so I paid a visit to the engine sheds and workshops at Pendre station, on the outskirts of Tywyn.

These engineering workshops are remarkable in themselves. They are the most extensive and the best equipped for forty miles, so they handle contract work for outside customers as well as maintaining the engines and coaches – farmers, local authorities, the Water Board, even other narrow-gauge railways. While I was there an engine wheel was being repaired for the Welshpool & Llanfair.

Wharf Station, Tywyn. No. 2, 'Dolgoch', prepares to depart.

The Talyllyn is unique in having a rail gauge of two feet three inches, which means it can't get the right size rolling-stock from other railways, but the workshops provide the answer. They are quite capable of adapting other stock to their gauge, or building their own. In fact they can tackle anything except major boiler repairs. John Bate, the chief engineer, is as remarkable as his workshop, capable of turning his hand to almost anything. Just before my visit he had helped a tug which was stranded at Aberdovey with a bent propellor. John Bate unbent it...

I met some more fascinating characters in the engine shed with tales to tell. One of them had a broad grin on its boiler and was being prepared for another children's outing, under the pseudonym of *Peter Sam*, a smaller cousin of Thomas the Tank Engine. Its real name was *Edward Thomas*, and by now it should have shed its disguise and be back on the normal Talyllyn service. Another engine in the shed had just been given a more permanent name. It started life with the

Opposite: *Emerging from the trees 'Dolgoch' enters Abergynolwyn Station.*

Exchange of single line token at Brynglas for 'Talyllyn'.

Opposite: 'Talyllyn' *approaching its final stop, Nant Gwernol Station. From here the fireman will uncouple the engine and transfer the headlamp to the back of the engine. 'Talyllyn' will then run around its train to prepare for the downhill trip to Tywyn.*

confusingly named Irish Turf Board, which has nothing to do with racing, it transports peat to the Irish power stations. When the Talyllyn society acquired it there was great pressure for calling it *Irish Pete*, but a formal vote was taken, tradition prevailed, and it was called *Tom Rolt* instead, after the society's founder.

The other character I found in the engine shed was Christine Homer, physics graduate, computer programmer – and lady fireman. I half-expected a formidable matron with muscles bulging out of greasy overalls, but Christine is young and slightly-built, and while her overalls were distinctly greasy, whatever bulges they displayed had nothing to do with muscles. She was cleaning an engine at the time, which I gathered was still her principal occupation on the Talyllyn, though she had been firing as well for the past four seasons.

Either occupation involves a lot of elbow grease as well as the oily sort, and the engine shed was even greasier and oilier than Christine. I just managed to stop myself asking the obvious question: 'What's a nice girl like you...' Instead I asked how she came to join the railway.

It was her husband Christopher who first brought her. They met at university and he took her to the Talyllyn during a vacation. Usually he worked in the engine shed too – though when I met him he was digging a drain at Tywyn Wharf station. There are few lines of demarcation among railway volunteers.

'It was the first time I'd seen a narrow-gauge railway, but when he asked me to come back again and help, I said I'd only come if I could join him in the locomotive department. He couldn't understand why I chose that; it turned out his sister didn't like getting her hands dirty, and he thought I'd be the same.'

Christine laughed at that, and so did I, though I could understand what he meant. Why *did* she want such a grubby job? The answer, it seemed, was quite simple.

'To me the attraction of a steam railway is the engines – so I wanted to work with the engines.' And she did.

It involved getting up extremely early to prepare the engine, oiling what needed oiling, polishing what needed polishing, and watching what the fireman did so she could learn to do it herself. She learned so successfully that in her third season she was given a firing trip, and when the season ended she got her 'passed cleaner' card. That meant she still got up extremely early, and still oiled and polished, but sometimes she was rostered to fire as well.

She and Christopher were married in the same year that she started work on the Talyllyn – 'he waited until he made sure I would come as a volunteer' – and they have gone there together every year since. Both of them are known as Chris, which can be confusing to a visitor, but most people know which is which...

I had to ask the question which I asked Lawrence Garvey in the signal box on Abergynolwyn station, and to which, as he had predicted, I had yet to be given a convincing answer. What is it, I wondered,

which attracts these volunteers from all over the country, not just to Talyllyn but to all the other Little Trains of Britain, to man lonely cabins on a hillside, or dig drains around a station, or get thoroughly filthy in an engine shed?

Some of the people I had asked talked of the friendliness, of the enjoyment of working as a team, of how married couples and indeed whole families could play a part together; one or two had mentioned its possibilities as a marriage bureau. But there had to be more to it than that, and at last, from Christine Homer, I got the answer.

She was talking about what it was like to work on the footplate. 'You can have a bad trip, when the pressure's down and the water's down and you're struggling to keep the fire going. But if you have a good trip, and everything goes right...'

Her face lit up under the smudges of grease, and although she may not have realised it, she was speaking for every volunteer on every little railway. 'There's only one word for it' – she held up her grubby hands to the sky in a gesture of supreme contentment – 'it's magic!'

And there was nothing more to say.

More Little Trains of Britain

Amberley Chalk Pits Museum

Houghton Bridge, Amberley, Arundel, W Sussex, BN18 9LT. Tel. (0798) 831370

Route: Amberley – Brockham, with industrial extension.
Distance: 500yd (passenger), 300yd (demonstration)
Gauge: 2 ft (also 100yd of 3 ft 2¼ in)
Service: During the period the Museum is open, normally Mar – Oct.

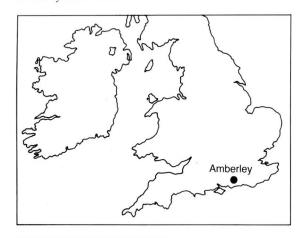

Amberley nestles in the South Downs of West Sussex, about midway between Pulborough and Arundel, and the chalkpits lie to the south of the village. Here can be found engines in a variety of narrow gauges, but there is more than just engines at Amberley. From the 1840s until the 1960s chalk was quarried and burnt in kilns here. Now a museum of the industrial history of southern England occupies a 36-acre site, of which working narrow railways of three types in two different gauges are an integral part. The longest, and the one most obvious from the entrance, is a 2ft-gauge main line, which runs from 'Amberley' to 'Brockham', along the north-west edge of the site. At both stations there are run-round loops, but beyond 'Brockham' the line becomes industrial, curving sharply round the north end of the complex. Crossing this is a short length of 3ft 2¼in gauge line, and there is another isolated stretch of this gauge serving the kiln area. A short length of industrial line at 2ft gauge branches from the main line at 'Amberley', running to the timberyard.

The Works Railway was established here in 1870, and was an important part of the Quarry's operation right up to closure. The Amberley Chalk Pits Museum opened on the site in 1979, and, by adding to the stock already held, now has over 30 locomotives of varying types, steam, petrol and electric, in 13 different gauges. A great boost in this respect was a merger with the Brockham Museum Trust in 1982, when that collection came to Amberley.

Notable among the engines are *Polar Bear* from the Groudle Glen Railway (qv), and *Townsend Hook* and *William Finley*, two of a handful remaining built by the Whitehaven firm of Fletcher, Jennings; of 3ft 2¼in gauge, they date from 1880. There is also a Decauville 0-4-0 well-tank, built in 1950 for the Chemin de Fer Touriste Foissy Domfriere, France. Passenger stock is typical of industrial railway accommodation, with examples from Penrhyn and Blaenau Ffestiniog (North Wales), RAF Fauld (Staffs), Colne Valley Water Co (Watford), with two 4-wheelers with reversible seats from Groudle Glen, and a bogie coach from the Rye & Camber Tramway. A replica Groudle Glen carriage is under construction, to form a 3-coach matching set.

At the industrial end is a large collection of diesel engines from brick and cement works, a water authority, the War Department, a sand railway, and a colliery, to name but a few. These range from a Simplex diesel to a machine for working under-ground, which disposed of poisonous exhaust gases through a system of water-filters. The scope of goods rolling stock is wide also, with examples from Dorset, North Wales, Bedfordshire and Kent among others. The aim is to acquire wagons from the same sources as locomotives, and in this the Museum has so far been largely successful. It is also an aim to expand the collection, in a field largely neglected by the preservation movement.

Audley End Steam Railway

Audley End, Saffron Walden, Essex, CB11 4JG. Tel. (0799) 41354/41956. (Enq. to: Estate Office, Buncketts, Wendon's Ambo, Saffron Walden, Essex, CB11 4JL).

Route: Return loop in Estate grounds.
Distance: 1.25 miles
Gauge: 10¼ in
Service: Daily Easter week, summer half-term, summer school holidays, otherwise Sat, Sun, BH mid-March – end-October.

Audley End House has been the home of the present Lord Braybrooke since 1946, and lies near Saffron Walden on the Essex/Cambridgeshire border. Lord Braybrooke has always been a steam enthusiast, and during the 1960s conceived the idea that a railway in the Audley End estate would be enjoyed by visitors coming to the House. Through Bassett-Lowke's he was put in touch with David Curwen of Devizes, who has since been responsible for much of the design and

Amberley Chalk Pits Museum

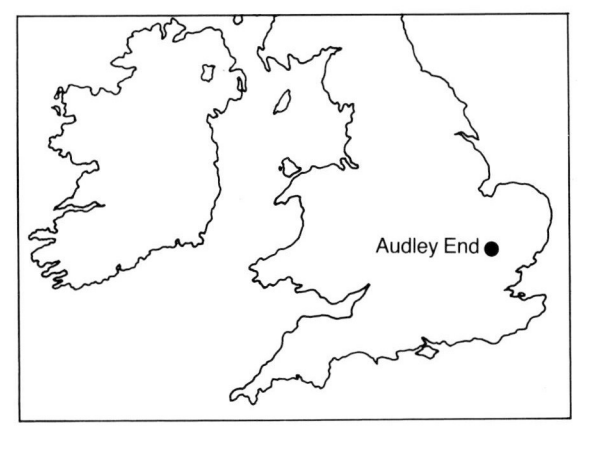

Audley End Steam Railway

building of Audley End's motive power.

Tracklaying began in 1963, on a site adjoining the coachpark for Audley End House. Full-sized sleepers were cut into nine (three cuts crossways, then three more lengthways) and laid at 18-inch intervals, with flat-bottomed rail spiked to them. There were no major earthworks other than a short cutting, and the first section of line was laid by Lord Braybrooke himself with estate staff. A Grand Opening, by Stirling Moss the racing driver, took place on 16 May 1964, when there were two engines to work the line – a second-hand Curwen 4-4-2 tender-engine (which in 1982 was rebuilt as a 2-6-2 and has now been named *Lord Braybrooke*) and a diesel, No D1011 *Western Thunderer*. Two sets of four articulated carriages were built in the Estate workshops and are still in service.

In August 1979 the line was extended to its present length, taking the form of an extended return loop. On leaving Audley End station the railway crosses first the River Fulfen, and then, almost immediately, the River Cam on a four-arch bridge built in the 19th century. At once the other end of the loop comes in on the left, but the train begins a short sharp climb at 1 in 42 to cross it, swinging north. Almost at once it turns the other way, climbing steadily to Gamage's Summit, before looping right and beginning a more gentle fall through the tunnel, which lies roughly at the halfway stage of the journey. Rounding a horseshoe bend the train reaches the bank of the Cam before curving away once more past Forest Deep Halt, to pass beneath the outward route. A long lefthand bend now takes it back to the riverbank, rejoining the outward route beside an old pillbox, relic of World War Two.

Beside the two locomotives already mentioned there are three other engines on the railway – another 4-4-2, No.4433 based on Ivatt's 1898 large-boilered design for the Great Northern Railway, and *Sara Lucy*,

a one-third scale model of the Denver & Rio Grande Railroad No.489. Livery closely follows that of the original, and so powerful is *Sara Lucy* that she has never yet been tested to her limit. She now has an American-style companion in *Linda*. *Doris* is a 0-6-0 freelance diesel, who also has a sister, a petrol-engined BoBo locomotive named *Henrietta Jane*.

Bala Lake Railway

The Station, Llanuwchllyn, Bala, Gwynedd, LL23 7DD. Tel. (067 84) 666

Route: Llanuwchllyn – Nr Bala
Distance: 4.5 miles
Gauge: 1 ft 11⅝ inches
Service: Daily end-March – end-September, weekends October.

When the Bala & Dolgelly Railway opened on 4 August 1868 it served nowhere of importance other than those towns. The most scenic part of the journey was at the Bala end, where the line skirted the

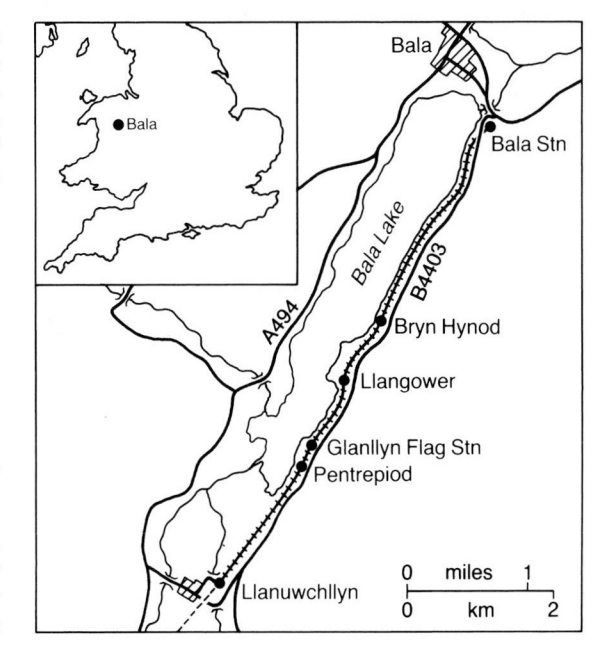

167

southern shore of the largest natural lake in Wales. On 15 January 1965 the line closed, and soon a scheme was being hatched to use the trackbed – by 1970 a line was proposed from Bala to Morfa Mawddach, on the coast near Barmouth (28 miles). This scheme suffered several prunings until a more practical size was reached , and the present Company was registered in 1972. Tracklaying began, the first 1.25 miles opening on 13 August that year, with another .75 miles to Llangower on 15 September. By 1976 the line had reached its present terminus, half a mile from Bala, and a passing loop at Llangower in 1979 increased capacity. Eventually it is intended to extend the line for about a mile by curving across the river Dee and round the foot of the lake to a new terminus beside the Bala/Dolgellau road.

Llanuwchllyn station, the headquarters of the BLR, is the last surviving Bala & Dolgelly Railway-built station on the old line thanks to George Barnes, whose brainchild the railway is. It has an added enhancement in the shape of a canopy made by the Cambrian railways at the turn of the century for its new station at Pwllheli. It was moved to Aberdovey in 1907, and on to its present site in 1979. Also acquired have been a seat from Liverpool Exchange, a waiting-room from Morfa Mawddach (now used as a cafe seating area), and bricks from Llandderfel.

One and a quarter miles of straight track (the longest on any narrow gauge railway in the country) brings the line to the lake shore. Glanllyn Halt has an ancient wooden building – when Sir Watkin Williams-Wynn arrived by train, a flag would be raised on a nearby pole to indicate to the staff at Glanllyn, his home on the opposite shore of the lake, that he required a ferry. Not perhaps surprisingly, Glanllyn Halt came to be known as Flag Station. Llangower is two miles from Llanuwchllyn, and is the main intermediate station; there is a passing loop, with a picnic site close by. After crossing a peninsula, the line now hugs the lake shore, past Bala Sailing Club, and runs into the terminus, ten minutes walk from the town.

The two steam engines of the BLR are both from Dinorwic Quarry in the north of the Principality (see also Llanberis Lake Railway) *Holy War* (1902) and *Maid Marian* (1903). The first came in 1976 after a short stay at Quainton Road, the second via periods of service at Bressingham (qv) and Llanberis from 1975. Both have been in regular service since. *Meirionydd* was built for the Railway in 1973, and *Chilmark* is a 1940 diesel mechanical from the RAF base of that name. The carriages number 10, six closed and four open, in a smart maroon and cream livery. The wagons are used for maintenance: six came from the RAF, and there are four side-tipping skips.

Beer Heights Light Railway

Pecorama, Beer, Nr. Seaton, Devon, EX12 3NA.
Tel. (0297) 21542

Route: long return loop.
Distance: 1 mile approx
Gauge: 7¼ in
Service: Daily: March – October, except Sat afternoon, Sundays: Easter – September

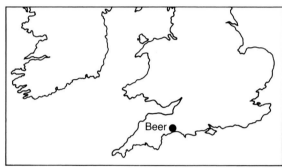

Beer lies a mile or two west of the Seaton Tramway (qv): on a spur of land high above the village can be found Pecorama, and within it a fascinating line well worth the climb to reach it. 1975 was the year in which the first train ran along the Beer Heights Light Railway. Local schoolchildren were carried free, and the opening train was waved away by the Rev W Awdry, creator of Thomas the Tank Engine. Since then the little line has gone from strength to strength. In those days it consisted merely of a return loop between Much Natter and Upsan Downs Junction, a short tunnel being included at the farthest corner of the loop. But since those days expansion has hit, hard. By gaining access to the opposite side of the ridge on which it is built, another long return loop, and a further loop within it, have extended the line to almost a mile in length, and a fascinating mile it is too.

Beginning at the terminus, the line passes beneath a foot-bridge and reaches Upsan Downs Junction, where, on the left, can be seen the engine shed, Now the line curves hard to the right, past the site of the original tunnel, before crossing a pond and running into White Falls station. It was here that the first line rejoined its outward route: not any more, for it now runs parallel with the outward line before swinging left into a substantial tunnel under the main carpark. This was opened in 1982, and brings the line out on the far side of the hill, where a right-hand curve around Mount Delight gives passengers a superb view over Lyme Bay. The line crosses itself and now takes course along a hillside area containing a nature trail.

Bala Lake Railway

Another right-hand curve follows, in a deep cutting, before the line crosses the nature trail and climbs back to the level of the outward route. After another circuit of Mount Delight, it plunges once more into the tunnel: on emerging, a sharp left-hand curve and a short cutting bring our train smoothly back into the terminus – and a remarkably smooth run it has been, too.

Six engines work the line – *Little Nell*, a diesel-electric unit, and *Thomas Junior* which worked the inaugural train, were the first. Since then have been added *Thomas II*, a smart red-liveried engine, *Dickie* who is black, *Linda* based on the ex-Penrhyn locomotive of the same name, now working on the Ffestiniog Railway, and a blue diesel named *Jimmy*. Carriages can seat four, and with six of them in the train, keep the queue for rides moving steadily.

And Pecorama has more than just the trains – models, gardens, children's activities and the nature trail among them.

Brecon Mountain Railway

Pant Station, Merthyr Tydfil, Mid-Glamorgan.
Tel. (0685) 4854

Route: Pant – Ponsticill
Distance: 2 miles
Gauge: 2 ft
Services: Steam trains, March – October, Santa trains in December.

The old Brecon and Merthyr Tydfil Junction Railway's line, from Brecon into South Wales, involved seven miles of climbing at 1 in 37 to Torpentau tunnel, the highest in Britain, after which the fall towards Merthyr was almost as steep. In 1964 BR closed what might justifiably have been described as the most spectacular line in Britain, and eight years later the owner of an engineering business in Llanberis conceived the idea of building a narrow gauge line in an area which did not already have one.

The site chosen was the trackbed of the old B&MTJR on the southern, or Merthyr, side of the ridge, from Pant, which lies north of that town, to Torpantau. There was no trouble about getting planning permission, but other preliminaries took

Beer Heights Light Railway

Brecon Mountain Railway

much time: when they had been gone through, a workshop, station, carpark and all the other amenities which make a tourist centre 'visitor-friendly' were built at Pant. The railway is laid for the most part on the trackbed of the old line, though a short diversion was necessary at Pant. Line construction began in 1978, and though delayed when an embankment was washed away in a storm on 29 December 1979, it opened to passengers in June 1980. At present it runs only as far as Ponsticill, but it is intended eventually to skirt the Taf Fechan reservoir and run through Torpantau tunnel to a new terminus at its north end high above Glyn Collwyn.

Of the seven engines at present on the strength, three come from Wales and five from overseas. Wales is represented by two vertical-boilered locos, both built in the north, and 1903-built *Sybil* from the Pen-yr-Orsedd Quarry, also in North Wales. This last was bought as scrap in 1963, and has been rebuilt. Three of the foreigners were built in Germany – *Graf Schwerin-Lowitz* comes from East Germany, and an incredible amount of time was spent rebuilding the engine. An Orenstein & Koppel 0-4-0 well-tank came from a Hamburg stone quarry, while No.77 is the most powerful locomotive ever built for the 2ft gauge, a 2-6-2 2-6-2 Garratt, built in Hanover. After working in Natal, South Africa from 1928 to 1965, it arrived in Wales on 18 March 1986, but is not yet in service. The 4-6-2 Baldwin, like the Garratt, worked in South Africa and was built in 1930. It will no doubt find service on the BMR something of a change after the cement works where it passed its previous life.

Stock for the passengers is home-built and distinctive, with a continental look which suits the motive power. They are square-bodied bogie carriages with end-balconies, and are painted in an attractive brown livery which blends well with the surrounding countryside. A recent addition, in traffic since Christmas 1989, is a scaled-down replica of a Sandy River & Rangeley Lakes Railroad caboose – as the only heated carriage on the line it is much in demand at Santa Special time.

Bressingham Steam Railway

Bressingham Steam Museum, Bressingham, Diss, Norfolk, IP22 2AB. Tel. (037 988) 382/386

Route: Three different routes within the Museum grounds.
Distance: Garden 750 yards, Nursery 2.25 miles, Waveney 2.5 miles.
Gauge: Garden 9½ in, Nursery 1ft 11 in, Waveney 15 in.

Service: Thur, Sun, BH, plus Wed in Jul & Aug. Museum open daily beg Apr – end Oct.

This site is not alone among those noted here as being more than simply a railway centre, for the main attraction to many is the superbly laid out garden. The whole complex can be found south of the A1066 Thetford to Diss road, 2.5 miles west of Diss.

There are no less than three lines here falling within the scope of this volume – let us take the smallest (and shortest) first, the Garden line. Straight, with a return loop at each end, it has but one engine, *Princess*, which is a 4-4-2 tender locomotive built in 1947. Smartly liveried in red, she came to Bressingham in 1965, and takes her passengers on a run through the pleasant house garden, out and back to the starting place.

The Waveney line is next in ascending order of gauge. This has an approximately square course, and for about a quarter of its length borders the River Waveney, the trains running clock-wise from a situation near the lake. The line in its present form was completed in 1974, and is powered by identical German tender-engines, 4-6-2s named *Mannertreu* and *Rosenkavalier*. They were built in 1937 and worked in pleasure parks in Dusseldorf, Munich and Cologne before reaching Bressingham in 1972.

The largest (in gauge at least) of the narrow-gauge lines at Bressingham is the Nursery line. It opened in

Bressingham Steam Railway

1966 as a mere half-mile run, but via subsequent extensions now gives passengers a much longer circuit. Running anti-clockwise, trains begin their journey near the main Museum building, cross the Waveney line twice, and return to the starting point by way of the Nurseries, through an area not otherwise accessible to the public. Four engines are available, all from the Penrhyn Quarries of North Wales. *Gwynedd*, built in 1885, and *George Sholto*, of 1909, are 0-4-0 saddle-tanks similar to *Lilian* (see Launceston Steam Railway), while *Bronllwyd* and *Eigiau* are both well-tanks and bigger.

George Sholto, slightly more powerful than *Gwynedd*, began the service on the Nursery Line, and after a second complete overhaul re-entered service in 1975 with a new boiler and firebox. *Bronllwyd* is a 0-6-0 built in Leeds in 1930 and rebuilt at Bressingham: it made its debut in 1969, bearing the brunt of the traffic for many years. *Gwynedd* was put to work in 1985, also after a complete overhaul, when she acquired a new boiler built in the Museum workshops. *Eigiau* is a 0-4-0 from Germany – as the only one of the quartet with a cab, she is less popular with train crews on hot days, and is kept as spare engine.

There is a standard-gauge steam museum at Bressingham too, as well as stationary and traction engines, and a new fire museum. The garden and Nursery complement the railway experience, making a worthwhile outing for those who find themselves in this part of Norfolk.

Bure Valley Railway

Aylsham Station, Norwich Road, Aylsham, Norfolk, NR11 6BW. Tel. (0263) 733858

Route: Aylsham – Wroxham
Distance: 9 miles
Gauge: 15 inches
Service: Daily: March – October, weekends: November – Christmas.

The Bure Valley Railway is perhaps the newest line in England, having opened only in 1990. Though planned earlier, it actually began to take shape in 1989, with a group determined to use part of the trackbed of the old East Norfolk Railway that had once run between Wroxham and Dereham. Passenger services along the line, opened in 1880, had closed in 1952, but BR had kept the formation in reasonable condition as an access route. A Light Railway Order was achieved, and the line was ready for a Gala Opening incredibly swiftly, on 10 July 1990.

The Bure Valley station at Wroxham adjoins that of

Bure Valley Railway

BR, to which it is linked by a footpath – indeed, a footpath accompanies the trackbed throughout its length – and has a three-track layout between two platforms, ending in a turntable. The narrow-gauge line diverges from its larger brother to the left, or west, soon crossing a road at Balaugh Green. A steady south-westerly curve and several bridges intervene before it reaches the first halt and passing-loop at Coltishall. The river comes close on the left now, and

will remain there until after the Little Hautbois passing-loop, the line eventually crossing it on a fine, 105-foot long, plate-girder bridge before reaching the second halt at Buxton Lamas. From here it is a short distance only to the next halt, on a new site at Brampton (the other stations/halts all had facilities in BR days), and it is here that the third passing-loop is sited. A comparatively easy run through farming country takes the line from Brampton towards Aylsham. A tunnel has been built beneath Aylsham's by-pass, where the old East Norfolk crossing-house still stands, and the main station on the line is entered soon after emerging. We have been rising gently but steadily since Wroxham, but gradients of 1 in 76 are necessary to carry the line beneath the road at Aylsham, which means that trains have a stiffish pull into the terminus there. The works/engine shed is at Aylsham (there is a viewing platform in the shed) and it is also the administrative centre for the line. For the first running season two steam locomotives were leased from the Romney, Hythe & Dymchurch Railway, and during that summer there were visiting engines from both Ravenglass and Bressingham. All helped to evaluate the power the BVR needs to work the line. In July 1991 a powerful 2-6-2 locomotive was acquired from the Fairbourne Railway. It required regauging, but already it has gone some way towards solving the power problem until such time as the BVR is in a position to build engines to its own design.

Now marketed as the 'Broadland line', a name chosen by competition, the BVR should provide a welcome alternative attraction in an area increasingly popular with visitors.

Dobwalls Forest Railroad

Dobwalls Family Adventure Park, Dobwalls, Nr. Liskeard, Cornwall.
Infoline: Tel. (0579) 20578/ 20325 /21129.

Route: Two intertwining circuits
Distance: 1 mile each circuit
Gauge: 7¼ in
Service: Daily Easter – end-September, weekends, school holidays November – Easter.

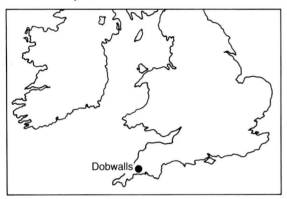

More than three million people will have travelled on the Dobwalls Forest Railroad by the time you read these words, no mean achievement for a line that opened its doors only on 23 May 1970. During the first year, services on the Forest Railway (as it was then called) were worked by locomotives of English outline, but severe curves and gradients – maximum 1 in 25 – took a heavy toll, and it was realised that something more powerful was required. A model of a Denver & Rio Grande 2-8-2 engine seemed the ideal solution, and so it has proved. Now renamed to suit its stock, the Railroad has collected ten American outline locomotives, six steam, four diesel. These are too numerous for individual justice to be done to them here, but No.488 *General Palmer* must be noted as the 2-8-2 which ran the 1971/2 service almost single-handed, not to mention much of the traffic for another six seasons. She/he now takes life more easily, but has topped 50,000 miles for all that, no mean feat for a 7¼in gauge machine.

Dobwalls Forest Railroad

No.88, now named after its builder, David Curwen, is the only 'freelance' loco, a 2-6-2 tender type, while No.4008 *William Jeffers* is a model of the largest steam locomotive ever built, the Union Pacific 4-8-8-4 *Big Boy*. Probably the most powerful engine of its gauge in the world, its full potential has never been tested on straight, level track, commodities in which Dobwalls does not proliferate. Large diesels are not forgotten either, in the Union Pacific 'Centennial' diesel-electric design, and in the twin-unit passenger diesel of the 1950s. Both these engines came from Severn-Lamb, in 1979 and 1983 respectively. The newest arrival from this maker (in 1989) is a 'cowl' diesel of the Atchison, Topeka & Santa Fe Railway. *Queen of Wyoming* (No.818) and *Queen of Nebraska* (No.838) were built in 1974 and 1981 respectively, and are both Union Pacific 4-8-4 designs. No.818 was reboilered in 1988, and No.838 had a heavy overhaul in 1989.

The line runs 48 identical bogie carriages, each loading 6-8 passengers, and trains are usually limited to seven vehicles on account of the stiff gradients and curves, though some of the engines are capable of handling considerably more.

The railroad is not the only attraction at Dobwalls, for its owner, John Southern's other passion is birds, and the site houses a Thornburn Gallery and Museum of Wildlife as well as woodland walks and play areas, the aim being to provide a family day out.

Locomotive maintenance in a service as intensive as that run at Dobwalls, with an average mileage of about 20,000 per engine, is more than £30,000 a year, while track on curved sections requires renewal about every eight months. But over three million passengers in 22 years is certainly a record to be proud of.

Foyle Valley Railway

Foyle Road Station, Derry City, BT48 6SQ.
Tel. (0504) 265234

Route: Through Foyle Road Urban Park.
Distance: about 0.6 mile
Gauge: 3 ft
Service: Apr – Sept, Tues – Sun, PH; Oct – Mar, Tues – Sat, Christmas, Easter.

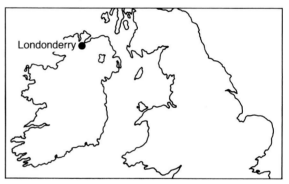

Compared with England and Wales, Ireland is less well-endowed with preservation projects. This particular scheme began in 1970, in an attempt to establish a museum and railway on the trackbed of the former Northern Counties Committee line from Victoria Road Station, Londonderry to Prehen, about three miles away.

In 1972 a Museum of artefacts from the local railway systems was opened at Victoria Road, the old NCC headquarters. It was shortlived however, for when, in 1979, the station came up for sale, the Council's bid was unsuccessful. Plans had to be abandoned, and the problem was only solved by the movement of the collection to Shane's Castle for safe keeping.

The railway also was difficult to bring about. An approach to Derry City Council for financial help was successful, and various sites were considered for the line. In the end it was decided that Foyle Road would be the most suitable, and construction of a purpose-built centre began in February 1985. Four years later, on 6 May 1989, Derry City Council was able to open its latest amenity, devoted mainly to the two largest of the Irish narrow-gauge systems, the County Donegal and the Londonderry & Lough Swilly Railways. The

Foyle Valley Railway

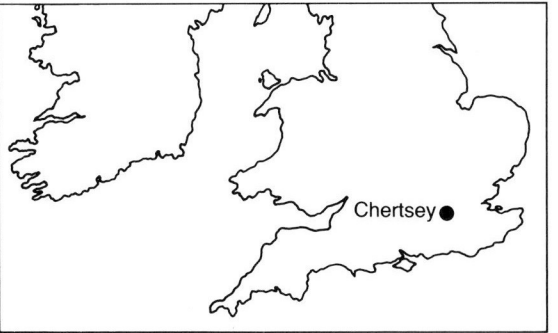

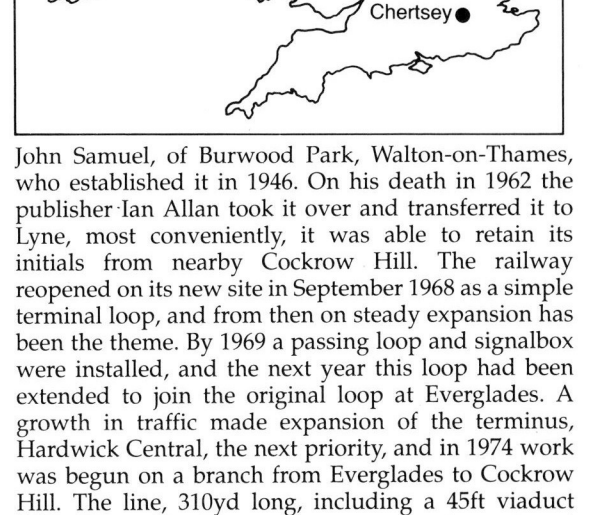

building is on the site of the Great Northern Railway (Ireland)'s old standard gauge – 5 feet 3 inches in Ireland – terminus, close to the double-decked Craigavon bridge, like that at Menai, having rail on the lower deck, with roadway above.

The Collection includes two steam locomotives, two railcars, two carriages and a railcar trailer, all from the CDR. Railcar No.1 is unique, and was built in 1906 – now affectionately known as 'The Pup', it was in service until 1947. The L&LSR is not quite so extensively represented, but a coach dating from 1880, at present undergoing restoration, is the prize item. There are several wagons on display, and the Clogher Valley Railway, the Dublin & Blessington Tramway and the Ballymena & Larne Railway are represented also.

The railway itself follows the trackbed of the old standard gauge line for some 900 metres, going through the pleasant Foyle Road Urban Park. The service is run by Railcar No.12, an ex-CDR vehicle, built in 1934. It once ran the 30-mile route between Strabane and Letterkenny, and clocked up over a million miles in doing so. Its run today is nothing like

so far, but it is hoped that in due course a terminus can be established at Carrigans, 6.5 miles away to the south-west, across the border. A river-bus service to Prehen Boat Club is also envisaged, with visitors able to return to Derry by vintage bus.

Great Cockrow Railway

Hardwick Lane, Lyne, Nr. Chertsey, Surrey.
Tel. (0932) 228950

Route: Hardwick Central-Cockrow Hill, and loops.
Distance: 2 miles of track
Gauge: $7^{1}/_{4}$ in
Service: Sundays 14.15 – 17.45, May – October.

Perhaps deliberately, for even on a not notably fine Sunday afternoon the carpark was well-filled and there was a 40-minute wait for a train-seat, this little line makes itself somewhat difficult to find. But it is well worth the search.

The line did not begin its life here. It was originally the Greywood Central Railway, and belonged to Sir

John Samuel, of Burwood Park, Walton-on-Thames, who established it in 1946. On his death in 1962 the publisher Ian Allan took it over and transferred it to Lyne, most conveniently, it was able to retain its initials from nearby Cockrow Hill. The railway reopened on its new site in September 1968 as a simple terminal loop, and from then on steady expansion has been the theme. By 1969 a passing loop and signalbox were installed, and the next year this loop had been extended to join the original loop at Everglades. A growth in traffic made expansion of the terminus, Hardwick Central, the next priority, and in 1974 work was begun on a branch from Everglades to Cockrow Hill. The line, 310yd long, including a 45ft viaduct across the main line and a stream on the outward journey, was opened in July 1979, but the single track section limited traffic. It was decided to build a separate return section and a tunnel, which involved the removal, by hand, of 200 tons of soil – work was begun in the winter of 1983/4, and the line opened in 1984. This is the present layout, but as the brochure notes, the line will never be complete, and there will always be a new project in hand somewhere. The railway is entirely self-supporting, all profits being ploughed back into improvement.

Seven or eight of the 23 locomotives listed in the brochure will probably be taking duty on any one day. Each of the 23 passenger vehicles seats four, most trains being made up of three vehicles, though a double-headed 'Gladesman' train, running twice on each working day, loads more. For a modest fare, visitors may use either a circuit route or the branch, while the 'Gladesman', with a premium fare, takes in both. Locomotives are reversed on the turntable at each terminus, though tender-first working was the practice from Great Cockrow until the turntable there had been installed. Carriages are green, except for one, which is Pullman brown. There are also 21 goods wagons.

Safety, as on any railway, must be paramount, and a comprehensive signalling system takes care of this.

173

Great Cockrow Railway

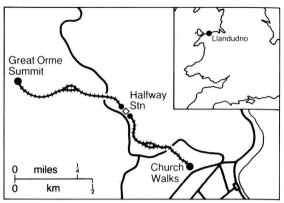

Semaphore signals are used at stations, but intermediate sections are controlled by colour-lights, and track-circuiting is installed too. There is a signalbox at each station, that at Everglades being equipped with a computer-based, four-character train describer. A recent addition at Hardwick Central has been the booking office from Ravenscourt Park on the District line, which is used for the same purpose here.

Great Orme Tramway

Victoria Station, Church Walks, Llandudno, Gwynedd. Tel. (0492) 870870 (Enq to: Grwp Aberconwy, Maesdu, Llandudno).

Route: Victoria Station – Great Orme Summit
Distance: 1.75 miles
Gauge: 3 feet 6 inches
Service: Daily, Apr – Sept inclusive.

Because of steep roads, contact between Llandudno town, established as a resort in 1849, and the headland of Great Orme was always awkward. By the 1880s the

influx of visitors sparked off suggestions for a funicular railway: local businessmen formed a Company to promote the idea, and on 23 May 1898, the Great Orme Tramways Act was passed. Cable-haulage was in mind from the start, trams working in pairs on separate upper and lower sections of track, driven by a central winding-house at Half Way Station.

Raising capital took some time, and building was not begun until April 1901. It was not until 31 July 1902 that the lower section opened for passengers. The line was a success at once, and 5000 people travelled during that initial bank-holiday weekend. Meanwhile work continued on the upper section, which was finally opened on 8 July 1903. Stray animals have always been a problem on this stretch, which has a maximum gradient of 1 in 10.3. A winter service was run on the lower section during 1902, but has not been repeated.

The first 25 years were prosperous, but a fatal accident caused a 21-month closure while a new fail-safe braking system was designed and tested: the line re-opened on 11 May 1934. It was sold in 1935 to a local syndicate, which operated it until Llandudno

UDR bought the line 14 years later. From 1 April 1972, as a result of Local Government re-organisation, Aberconwy Borough Council assumed responsibility, and in 1990 Grwp Aberconwy, the commercial department of the Council, took over maintenance and operation. The overhead wire and hand-cranked telephone system was replaced with radio-control between the cars and the winding-house. A new livery for the cars and uniforms for the staff was also introduced, together with improved station facilities.

Four original tramcars survive – they have a 30ft saloon and two open end-platforms, the overall width of each car being 7ft 6in. The cars seat 48 and run on two bogies. Power is an electric motor, the trams being cable-hauled. Cars 4 and 5 carry emergency skid-brakes, which automatically contact the road if a speed of 5mph is exceeded. The original slipper-brakes are sufficient on the upper, easier section, where the maximum speed is 7mph.

Victoria station is the bottom terminus, from which the line rises 400ft in 872yds, the steepest pitch of an average gradient of 1 in 6 being 1 in 4. The line runs along the centre of the road at first, before crossing to

Great Orme Tramway

enter its own route. The upper section, is shorter, at 827yd: it rises 150ft in this distance, on its own private right of way. There is one level crossing, of the road to St. Tudno's Church.

Views from the 679ft summit are magnificent. On a clear day the Isle of Man and Blackpool Tower can be seen, while closer at hand Snowdonia, Anglesey and the Conwy estuary provide memorable panoramas.

Groudle Glen Railway

Groudle Glen, Onchan, Isle of Man.
Tel. (0624) 622138 (eve only)

Route: Lhen Coan – Sea Lion Rocks
Distance: 0.5 mile
Gauge: 2 ft
Service: Easter w/e, BH Mons, Suns end-May – end-September.

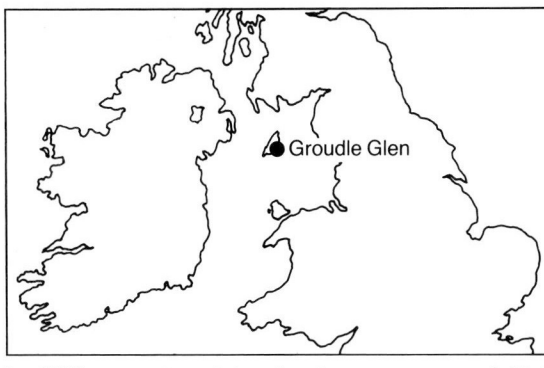

In 1893 an enterprising businessman named R M Broadbent had the idea of developing for tourists to the Isle of Man, an area north of Douglas called Groudle Glen. A path led through the glen to a rocky headland, where an inlet was dammed: as an attraction, sealions were introduced into the resulting pool, and in 1895, to provide an added incentive for visitors, work began on a 2ft gauge railway between the upper area of the glen and the 'Headland Zoo'. The 0.75-mile line was finished in the spring of 1896, and three passenger coaches were delivered, along with a 2-4-0 steam engine named *Sea Lion*. The first passengers travelled on 23 May, and the line was an immediate success. Extra carriages were ordered, and in May 1905 a second engine, *Polar Bear*, arrived.

After World War One, when the line was closed, battery locomotives ran the service, but these were worn out after six years and the steamers returned to work. The line closed again in World War Two, but after this a decline set in. Vandalism and a landslip did not help, and an intermittent service from 1950 to 1961

Groudle Glen Railway

culminated in closure the following year. In 1966 *Polar Bear* went to the Brockham Museum Association (see Amberley Chalk Pits Museum), but *Sea Lion* remained on the Isle of Man at first, before moving to Loughborough.

Polar Bear and *Sea Lion* were built in Stafford, and are identical except that some of the former's dimensions are greater than her sister's – cylinder size and wheel diameter, for example, and a firebox of 60 square feet instead of 52. The battery locos arrived in March 1921 and were the first engines of this type to be used on any British narrow gauge passenger line. They were converted to 2-4-2, but this was not a success, despite being given a four-wheeled tender in which the batteries were carried. Neither is thought to have survived longer, possibly, than 1929.

In 1982 the restoration of the railway was begun by volunteers. There was much work to do. On 4 March 1983 *Sea Lion* came home, and the engine's restoration began, later being completed under a British Nuclear Fuels Ltd apprentice training project. The line now has two 4-wheeled diesel engines, which have been given steam outlines and christened *Dolphin* and *Walrus*.

Built by Hunslet of Leeds in 1952, they came to Groudle in March 1983. On 18 December that year, the first public trains for 21 years ran, and development slowly went forward. On 25 May 1986 the line was officially re-opened, and further steady progress followed. *Sea Lion* steamed in the glen again on 21 September 1987, and now plans are in hand, with rail bought from the Stoke Garden Festival in 1988, to relay the line to Sea Lion Rocks. At the time of writing, this extension is scheduled for a 1992 re-opening.

Great Whipsnade Railway

Whipsnade Wild Animal Park, Dunstable, Beds, LU6 2LF. Tel. (0582) 872171

Route: A circuit within animal paddocks
Distance: 2 miles
Gauge: 2 feet 6 inches
Service: During normal opening times

In 1970/71 Pleasurerail built the Whipsnade & Umfolozi Light Railway as a means of carrying the

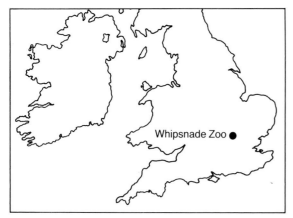

public closer to the animals of Whipsnade Zoo, high on Dunstable Downs, in particular the herd of white rhino. These had come from the Umfolozi Game Reserve, hence the Railway's name. In 1985 however, the park's authorities decided to move the rhino away from the line, and the name became redundant: the line was rechristened the Great Whipsnade Railway,

whose initials, it will be noted, are famous in a wider railway sphere. In 1990 Pleasurerail was bought out by Zoo Operations Ltd, the undertaking which runs the park at Whipsnade.

The line runs through paddocks of yak, camel and deer. The station stands near the dolphinarium, and the train, if travelling in a clockwise direction, passes through a small cutting before crossing a road on the level, about a quarter of a mile from the start. Another cutting follows, and then the line swings sharply right, leaving the entrance to the engine sheds on the left. The line is crossing open country now, and soon after bearing right again, crosses a pond, from which a straight section leads to the halfway point.

After crossing a second pond the line swings right again, and a substantial embankment carries it across a stream. The line now follows the valley of this stream for a short distance before plunging once more into a cutting and bearing left to another level-crossing. Then, with a sharper right-hand curve, still in a cutting, the line emerges to skirt a large pool. A major walkway now runs on the left, and shortly afterwards we reach our starting place once more.

Most of the equipment comes from the Bowaters Papermill Railway in Kent (see Sittingbourne & Kemsley Railway) – *Chevallier* is a 0-6-2 side-tank built in 1915. *Excelsior*, a 0-4-2 saddle-tank and *Superior* a 0-6-2 side-tank, were both built in Stafford in 1908 and 1920 respectively, while *Conqueror* (which had the misfortune to fall into the dock at Bowater's during the 1953 floods) dates from 1925. Steam operation is normally used, but shunting and the passenger service in off-peak periods is covered by two diesels, *Victor* and *Hector*, built in 1951.

Passengers are carried in a fleet of 15 coaches, built on pulpwagon bogie frames, but it is hoped, in the near future, to be able to acquire several items of Polish rolling-stock, so that the capacity of the line can be increased. The zoo is extremely popular, and the railway, at peak times, is very busy. A question the staff are often asked by visitors is whether the trains disturb the animals. The answer is quite the contrary – when the rhinos were in the paddock, engine crews often had to persuade the animals that between the rails was not the safest place to sleep!

Hythe Pier Railway

Hythe, Hampshire. Tel. (0703) 843203

Route: Along the southern side of Hythe Pier.
Distance: 700 yards approx
Gauge: 2 feet
Service: 0700-2000 daily ex Sunday/BH, Sunday/BH (ex Christmas Day) 0900-1700.

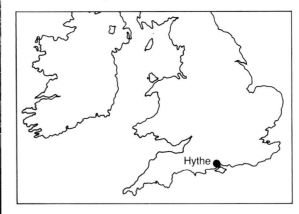

Very few of the railways noted in these pages can claim to be run primarily as a public service rather than a tourist or visitor attraction. To be sure, this railway encourages visitors, advertising the fact that from the Ferry is the best place to see the big ships on Southampton Water – and why not, for it is.

Great Whipsnade Railway

Hythe Pier Tramway

Hythe Pier stretches into the western side of Southampton Water just south of the village's marina, and slightly nearer to Fawley than to Totton. It is about half a mile long, and a regular ferry service to Southampton Town Quay runs from the end of it. The Hythe Pier Railway connects the shore with the ferry. Each half-hour (that at least was the time interval in August 1991) the little three-coach train, smartly painted in blue and white and powered by a small electric locomotive, sets off for the pier-head with a complement of passengers. These it will exchange for those of the ferry's payload who wish to ride back along the pier to the village. Then it rests until the next boat is due.

Hythe Pier was opened on 1 January 1880, and plans for a railway were put forward when the pier scheme was first mooted, as far back at 1870. But it was not until July 1909 that a tramway was laid, the idea being that a hand-propelled trolley could be used to take luggage to the ferry and bring luggage and cargo to the shore – the wheels of the trolleys already in use were damaging the planking of the walkway. The tramway was a success at once. Further sidings developed over the years, and in July 1922 an electric railway was introduced. It worked on the three-rail system, the live rail, for the purposes of safety, being on the side of the track furthest from the pedestrian way along the pier.

There were originally three locomotives (built for factory use at Avonmouth, Bristol), one of which has now been dismantled to provide spares for the remaining pair, and the three carriages were at first painted green and cream. During WW2 the train was used by King George VI during a visit to shore bases in the area shortly before D-Day, and it made further history in October 1962 when it was the only railway running on the first day of a national strike. There was a more recent occasion too, in 1980, when the train crew showed a great presence of mind by lowering buckets to collect seawater to put out a fire on the pier.

So, quite apart from the fine views from both pierhead and water, many daily commuters can save themselves a lengthy drive and considerably time by using this little line. Certainly it can be aptly described as a 'very useful railway'.

Launceston Steam Railway

St. Thomas Road, Launceston, Cornwall, PL15 8DA. Tel. (0566) 775665

Route: Launceston – New Mills
Distance: 2 miles
Gauge: 1ft 11⅝in
Service: Easter – October, with seasonal variations.

If you travel by car to visit the Launceston Steam Railway, you may very well park it on the site of the old London & South Western Railway station, opened in 1886. The L&SW line was extended in stages to Padstow, which it finally reached on 27 March 1899,

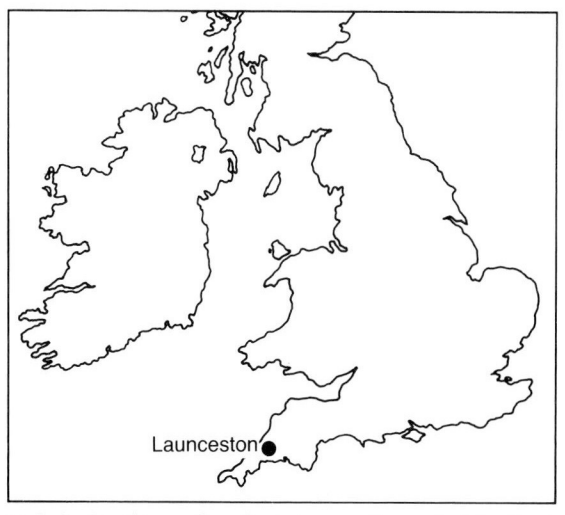

and it is along the first two miles of this line's trackbed, closed by British Railways in October 1966, that Nigel Bowman and his colleagues have laid track to a gauge of 1ft 11⅝in.

Launceston Steam Railway

Mr Bowman was a teacher for a short time before returning to his first love, engineering. In 1964 he found *Lilian,* a 0-4-0 Hunslet saddle-tank built in 1883, abandoned in Penrhyn quarry, North Wales. Having rebuilt her he needed somewhere to run her, and, aware of redundant trackbeds in the West Country, wrote on spec to Launceston Town Council. The Council supported him from the start, and though much time was lost in legal wrangles, track was eventually laid for a short distance westwards along the Kensey valley from Launceston. It opened on 26 December 1983.

The line begins in a cutting, and soon after leaving the station (whose canopy comes from Tavistock North) passes beneath a minor road bridge, originally built wide enough for double track should it have become necessary. It never did. Next comes an attractive aqueduct which carries the stream for the Town Mills across the railway, and the line then leaves the cutting and runs on to embankment, still climbing at 1 in 110. A two-arch masonry bridge takes the track across the river Kensey, and the countryside becomes more open. This was the line's limit at opening, but it has now, via extensions opened in 1986 and 1989, reached New Mills, where there is a picnic site. A further two-mile extension is planned.

Mainstay of the steam service is the aforementioned *Lilian,* now ably assisted by *Covertcoat,* another Hunslet (built 1889) saddle-tank but this time from the Dinorwic quarries. They were joined late in 1987 by *Velinheli* and *Sybil,* again from Dinorwic and built in 1886 and 1906 respectively. The rusting remains of a fifth engine, *Dorothea,* built in 1901, have just arrived to join them, and will form the next restoration project.

All the carriages are replicas, Nos.1 and 3 of Manx Electric Railway trailer cars, though No.3 has certain modifications. No.67 is of a carriage which ran on the short-lived Torrington & Marland line in North Devon early this century, and will shortly be joined by a Plynlimon & Hafan carriage. Other rolling stock consists of L&NW and Ffestiniog wagons, and ex-Admiralty box-vans. Rail has come from various places, the oldest being stamped 1872. The next project is to create a replica of the Brennan Monorail.

Leadhills Light Railway

The Station, Leadhills, Lanarkshire.
Tel. A Smith (041 556) 1061

Route: Leadhills towards Glengonnar
Distance: ⅓ mile
Gauge: 2 ft
Service: Variable – telephone for details

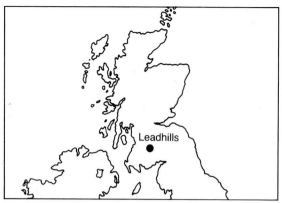

Leadhills station stands at an altitude of 1405ft – not the most obvious or convenient of places to put a light railway, one might think, but in spite of this the Leadhills Light Railway is actually the second line to have a station on the site. The first was the Leadhills & Wanlockhead Light Railway, a branch built by the Caledonian Railway westward from Elvanfoot on its main line, to serve leadmines at the two places named. In an attempt to encourage tourism, passengers were carried too, and the line opened as far as Leadhills on 1 October 1901 and on to Wanlockhead a year later. Between the two villages the line reached the height of 1498ft, making it the highest adhesion-worked line in the UK – Druimuachdar summit on the Highland Railway fell a few feet below this, at 1484ft. The leadmines closed in the 1930s however, and, since freight traffic had always been more important to the line than passengers, it now had little future. The final train ran on 31 December 1938, and early the following year the track was lifted.

Leadhills Light Railway

The Lowthers Railway Society, which is now resuming operations on a tourist basis in these remote but attractive uplands, is a young group formed in 1983. A long legal battle over the trackbed was eventually resolved by BR, and there was a setback when an application for grant-aid failed. Just as the lease was finalised, 30 tonnes of rails, a diesel locomotive (in numerous parts), and two wagons were acquired from the sale of a private railway in Norfolk, and tracklaying began on the bed of the old railway between Leadhills and Wanlockhead in 1986. In due course 600 yards of mainline track plus sidings attained Railway Inspectorate approval, and a service began, run by three of the five diesels presently owned by the group. Steam returned, albeit temporarily, on 18/19 August 1990 using the Kerr Stuart 0-4-0 saddle-tank *Peter Pan,* on loan for the occasion. The event was repeated over a quarter-mile of track in 1991, again with great success. Development of a carpark and station facilities have continued at Leadhills, and it is hoped that a permanent steam loco can be acquired for the line, which offers a challenging ruling gradient of 1 in 40.

Extension of the line to Glengonnar is in hand, and a signalbox has been acquired from Tulloch, on the West Highland line. It is planned that this will be rebuilt in operational form at Leadhills. The Lowthers Railway Society (which runs the line) is going through the pioneer period which most other lines noted here have passed. There is some way to go, but their progress will be watched with interest.

Lightwater Valley Light Railway

Lightwater Valley Theme Park, North Stainley, Ripon, N. Yorks, HG4 3HT. Tel. (0765) 635321

Route: continuous loop within the Theme Park
Distance: slightly over a mile
Gauge: 15 inches
Service: Easter – Oct. Variable – telephone for details.

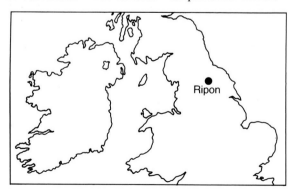

Lightwater Valley Theme Park lies to the west of the A6108 between Ripon and Masham, about three miles north of Ripon. The railway is part of a much larger leisure complex, and acts as a link between many of the attractions. There are three stopping-places: Lightwater Station, near the main entrance, Fort William, which serves the children's adventure park, and Whistle Stop, lying close to the boating lake and the two roller-coaster rides. Passenger accommodation is in/on flat vehicles furnished with transverse seats, and there are four different steam engines available to work the trains. *Royal Scot* is based on the LMS locomotive of the same name, the original of which can be seen at Bressingham (qv), while *Yvette* is to a freelance design. Two Bassett-Lowke engines complete the working roster, and are named *Little Giant* and *King George*, while also on view are *Blacovesley*, a Bassett-Lowke petrol engine, and a steam crane. Locomotives and crane are housed beside the main station at Lightwater, in a spacious four-road shed built in traditional 1860s style. During off-peak periods the railway service is run by a convincingly steam-outlined diesel *Rio Grande*, built by Severn-Lamb.

The train sets out on its journey, travelling clockwise from Lightwater Station, first rounding the foot of the lake, and passing close to the main entrance gates. It then heads south along the eastern side of the water, with woods rising to the left. Fort William lies near the head of the lake, and is the stop for the children's adventure playground, after which the line curves to the right. Giant swingboats loom above the trees to the left now, while on the right competitors on the Grand Prix Karting rink dice with each other on the race track.

Now beyond the head of the lake the train moves out on to an embankment, bridges a path, and swings sharp right into Whistle Stop. Behind and to the left are the roller-coasters, and the boating lake lies to the right. The curve continues through a deep cutting and into a short tunnel: beyond it there is a brief glimpse of the lake to the right before the line takes the only substantial left-hand turn on its route. All too soon it is crossing the tail-end of the Devil's Cascade (a watersplash ride) and re-entering Lightwater station once more.

Lightwater is home to other steam exhibits too. There is a substantial collection of traction engines, steam rollers and showman's engines, along with fairground engines, a 'Galloping Horses' carousel and threshing machines, are usually on display at weekends. In September each year a grand Steam Gala is held – with all this space available, one feels it must be quite a sight.

Lightwater Valley Light Railway

Lincolnshire Railway Museum

Station Yard, Burgh-le-Marsh, Lincs, PE24 5EZ.
Tel. (075 485) 347

Route: Return loop
Distance: 0.5 mile
Gauge: 10¼ in
Service: Regular during opening hours, which vary seasonally.

The miniature line at the Lincolnshire Railway Museum, it must be said at once, is but part of a project in a much wider context. It began as a scheme for volunteers at the former site of the Museum at Kirton-in-Lindsey, in North Lincolnshire, but has now developed, in the words of Director, Alan Turner, into '... a valuable support for the Museum'. The railway became established at Kirton in the mid-70s, but quickly outgrew its site, and in 1987 moved southwards to its present Burgh-le-Marsh location, south of the A158 half a mile east of the Gunby roundabout. Here, just five miles from the popular holiday centre of Skegness, it occupies the site of the yard and station once owned by the East Lincolnshire Railway, whose station at Burgh, on the line from Grimsby to Boston, was opened on 4 September 1848. The Great Northern Railway leased the line and worked it throughout its independent life, which ended when the Company became an LNER subsidiary at the Grouping on 1 January 1923.

The Museum is housed in the old goods shed and yard, but the site also has its own wildflower and conservation area, where 400 native trees have been

Lincolnshire Railway Museum

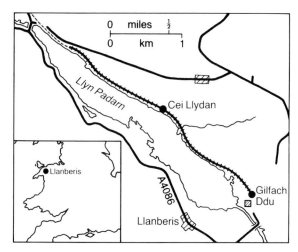

planted to give added enhancement. The present line runs for about half a mile through this area, which is not normally accessible on foot, and partly alongside Gunby Park, a National Trust property. From the old terminus in the goods dock, the line passes the goods shed and a replica of a Ffestiniog Railway two-armed signal. It is from here that the new loop will run, off to the left. Swinging sharply right, the line crosses ponds created to widen the scope of the plant and animal life on the site. Then, curving left again, the trees of Gunby Park stand on the right, and in a little while the loop can be seen re-entering on the left. A short tunnel is reached, and the line curves left to rejoin the outward route before crossing the ponds again and so running back to the terminus. A deliberate (and successful) attempt has been made to enhance the narrow gauge atmosphere for visitors, and though the three locomotives which cater for the passenger traffic are motor-powered, two, *Goth* and *Volunteer* have an extremely convincing steam outline.

Projects, as always with establishments of this sort are on-going. The extension is already under way, and will use a building from the GCR halt at Barrow Haven, near New Holland as part of a second return loop instead of the present (1991) terminus. This was rescued and used at Kirton, but is now dismantled and awaiting reconstruction. It is planned also to create a new siding space with storage buildings, which will increase the capacity of the line, the new loop making operation much easier at busy times. Mr Turner says he would have liked to re-establish the Museum in a larger area, but this is now unlikely.

'So we work,' he says, 'as if we are here for ever.' The many visitors who have enjoyed days here, will wish him well.

Llanberis Lake Railway

Padarn Country Park, Llanberis, Caernarfon, Gwynedd, LL55 4TY. Tel. (0286) 870549

Route: Gilfach Ddu (Llanberis) – Penllyn
Distance: 2 miles
Gauge: 1 ft 11½ in
Service: March – October except Saturdays, July – August daily.

When engineers built a 4ft-gauge railway to bring slate to the Menai Straits at Y Felinheli (later Port Dinorwic) from quarries near Llanberis, the only way to do it was by a shelf cut a few feet above the waters of Llyn Padarn. This became the Padarn Railway, which in 1843 superseded an earlier, horse-worked tramway running at a much higher level. The Padarn was probably horse-worked too, at first, but steam was introduced in 1848 – one of the engines *Fire Queen* and other items of stock can be seen at nearby Penrhyn Castle, owned by the National Trust.

The line closed in October 1961 and rapidly reverted to nature, until closure of the quarries eight years later provided both the stock and the inspiration for a narrow gauge line along the old trackbed. Work began in 1970, and in July the next year a run of a mile opened to Cei Llydan (Kay Thlid-Ann). The full two miles to Penllyn were inaugurated in 1972.

The line is run by three steam engines, *Elidir* (1889), *Wild Aster* (now renamed *Thomas Bach*) built in 1904, and *Dolbadarn* (1922), similar Hunslet saddle-tanks, though all have detail differences: all once worked in the quarry here. Trains run every half-hour from late morning during the peak season. The carriages are of various types, used according to the weather. There are 13 in all, five closed, two part-closed and six open: all were mainly built in the workshop beside the Quarry Museum. Incidentally, this Museum will more than repay a visit, but make sure you have plenty of time – it is very easy to lose track of it once inside!

But back to the railway journey. Soon after departure the train runs into a steep-sided cutting crossed by a high arch, and beyond it the views open out once more. That across the lake towards Llanberis is unimpeded other than by an occasional tree. Heron can

Llanberis Lake Railway

sometimes be seen fishing in the lake, and Allt Wen woods, on the opposite side of the line, are home to a wide variety of wild life. At Cei Llydan there is a picnic site, but the train will stop here only on the return journey.

Volcano Cutting, a short way beyond the station is made through solidified strata. The slate building just past here on the right houses machinery and equipment connected with the enormous hydro-electric plant now built inside the mountain, beneath the old slate galleries. At Penllyn station, about a quarter of a mile short of the foot of the lake, passengers may not leave the train, but the views can be enjoyed from the train while the engine changes ends for the return journey. The wait is sometimes all too short, for the lake can be an impressive sight, even in bad weather.

Manx Electric Railway

Derby Castle, Douglas, Isle of Man.

Route: Douglas – Ramsey
Distance: 17.75 miles
Gauge: 3 feet
Service: Daily, Easter to late September

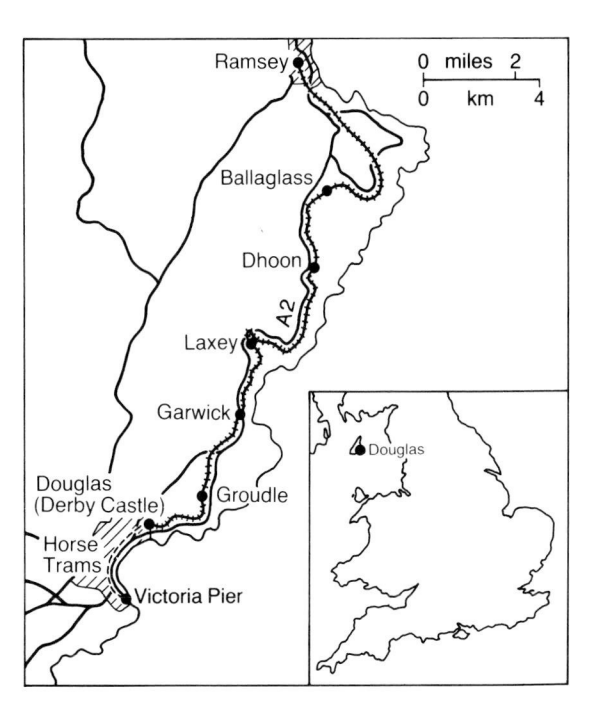

Once upon a time there were two railways linking Douglas, the 'capital' of the Isle of Man, with Ramsey, the largest place in the north of the island. One was worked by steam, the other by electricity. Had the steam line managed to hold on into the preservation era it would surely be going still – unfortunately it didn't, so only the electric line has survived.

The Manx Electric Railway began life as a 2.5-mile single-line tramway, opened in the late summer of 1893 as the Douglas & Laxey Coast Electric Tramway. By the following year the track had doubled and an extension opened to a station in Laxey, south of Glen Roy. Construction of a further extension to Ramsey began in 1896, and the completed line was opened on 24 July 1899. It cost, of course, much more than anticipated, and bankrupted its Company: like the Snaefell line, it had a number of owners before the Isle of Man Government bought it is 1957.

The terrain of the east coast is much harder than that of the west, and a route along it involved steep gullies which needed bridging, sharp curves, and gradients as steep as 1 in 24. The average distance between stops is 550 yards, but many of these are seldom-used. The line begins at Derby Castle, at the north end of Douglas Promenade, and at once climbs steeply away towards Onchan Head. The climb is followed by a level section and a descent, to Groudle where another climb begins to Baldrine. Then come Ballabeg and Laxey, where there is an interchange with the Snaefell Mountain Railway, and a dual-gauged siding used when the Snaefell cars need maintenance. Three-foot gauge bogies are slid beneath the wider car, which then proceeds to Douglas under its own – well, not steam, but power, anyway.

The line now climbs eastwards away from Laxey, turning north at Laxey Head, but still climbing, to a 550-foot summit and a superb view-point above Bulgham Bay. Inland now through Dhoon Glen, but the line winds back seaward through a deep cutting spanned by a high bridge at Corrony, through Ballaglass and Cornaa to Dreemskerry. From this point near Maughold Head the line begins to descend through Lewaigue and Ballure, eventually reaching its Ramsey terminus, near the town-centre, after a circuitous but fascinating journey. Much of the route, particularly in the south half of the line, is along roadside, though there are some lengthy stretches of private way.

The rolling-stock is varied, but divides basically into driving- and trailer-cars. Most date from 1893–1906, though three of the trailer-cars had to be replaced in 1930 after a fire at Laxey. Capacity and the configuration of the seating varies too – in some cars it is longitudinal, in some transverse. Power does not

Approaching Laxey Station, Manx Electric Railway.

Douglas Horse Tram

vary however: it is all by overhead cable, and the journey is impressive however variable the weather.

In addition to the electric railway a horse-drawn tram operates from Derby Castle, along Douglas promenade to Victoria Pier. This was opened in August 1876 before the coming of the electric railway. The stables for the horses are situated near to Derby Castle station and are well worth a visit.

Mull & West Highland Narrow Gauge Railway

Old Pier Station, Craignure, Isle of Mull, PA65 6AY. Tel. (06802) 494

Route: Craignure Pier – Torosay Castle
Distance: 1.25 miles
Gauge: 10¼ in
Service: Easter, then end-April – mid-October.

Laxey Station, Manx Electric Railway.

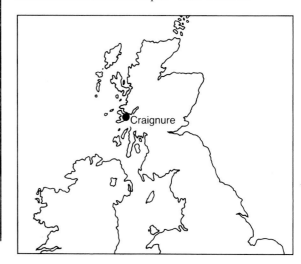

One might be forgiven for wondering why, having survived for a century and a half without a railway, Mull should now decide that it needs one. But the reason is easily found – when, in 1975, Torosay Castle and its gardens were thrown open to the public, some sort of transport between the pier at Craignure and the grounds became essential – this little railway has filled the necessity in the best way possible.

It was a while, however, before it happened. Though a decision to build was made in 1975, planning permission had to be obtained and local objections overcome, so that it was April 1982 before the project was actually started. The two main problems were opposites – a summit and a bog. Building began from the Castle end, and the summit was the first obstacle, conquered by blasting and a shallow cutting. The bog was more difficult to deal with, but was overcome with Scotlay, a modern version of the birch mats which helped Stephenson across Chat Moss. Craignure was duly attained by February 1983.

On 22 May that year *Lady of the Isles*, a 2-6-4 side-tank built in 1981, was steamed for the first time and busied herself with ballast wagons, working out of Craignure, since that was where the ballast stockpile lay. An experimental service began that August, and an official opening took place on 22 June 1984, by Chris Green (then General Manager of Scotrail) and his wife Mitzi.

There are four locomotives on the line at present. *Lady of the Isles*, a 2-6-4 tank-engine, is resplendent in North British livery, and spent two years on loan at Kessingland, Suffolk before coming to Mull, while *Waverley* is a 4-4-2 tender-engine built in 1948, and first used on the Weymouth Railway. It travelled extensively after that, but was bought from the North Midland Railway at Loughborough in 1975 for use on Mull. It is presently undergoing overhaul and will emerge in Perth Caledonian blue. *Prince* is based on the Class 26 type diesel which made itself almost synonymous with Scottish railways – it was built for the North Midland Railway. *Glen Auldwyn* is a home-built engine, powered by a Perkins diesel. Three of the eleven carriages also came from the North Midland, but have been rebuilt at Torosay – five more, to a similar pattern, have been built from scratch, and the rest were acquired in 1990.

The line begins at Craignure Pier and follows the shoreline to Tarmstedt, named after the narrow-gauge station from which the owner of Torosay Castle made two wartime escapes. By now the train has crossed the bog, and descends almost to sea level before attacking Beattock, the line's high point, reached after a gradient of 1 in 52-74 for about 90 metres. Then comes a sharp

Mull & West Highland Narrow Gauge Railway

drop of 50 metres at 1 in 72 into Skeleton Gulch, followed by a steepish but shorter climb out. The terminus is but a short step from the front door of Torosay Castle.

Seaton Electric Tramway

Riverside Depot, Harbour Road, Seaton, Devon EX12 2NQ. Tel. (0297) 21702/20375

Route: Seaton-Colyton
Distance: 3 miles
Gauge: 2 feet 9 inches
Service: Daily, Good Friday – end September. Limited winter service.

The Seaton and Beer Railway never reached Beer, and having driven the road between the two places one can see why! The line opened as a branch to the South Devon coast at Seaton from Seaton Junction on 16 March 1868, and though it made a modest living, never became a moneyspinner. In 1885 the L&SWR took over from the independent Company, but during

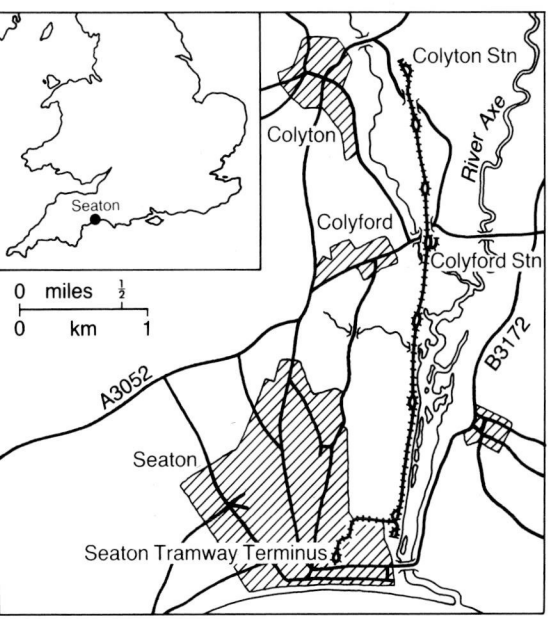

Seaton Electric Tramway

the 1930s traffic fell off in the face of road competition. The 1960s brought Dr. Beeching, and when the last passenger left the station at Seaton Junction on 7 March 1966, a history of rail travel between that place and the coastal town came to an end after almost a century. And yet...

In Eastbourne there was a Company called Modern Electric Tramways Ltd, where it ran a highly successful tramway. But from 1964 doubts about the Eastbourne site began to concern the Directors, and a move elsewhere was mooted. Negotiations were slow, but finally, on Christmas Eve 1969, the Company obtained a Transfer Order. The move to Seaton took place during 1970, and by the start of the 1971 season a mile of single track had been laid along the trackbed of the old Seaton branch railway. The work continued until, on 23 September 1973, the new overhead system was used for the first time. The terminus at this time was near the old railway terminus, but now a diversionary extension was made round around a holiday camp area to a new site nearer the seafront and the shops, and with more space. This opened on 17 May 1975, and the extension at the other end, to Colyton, was fully opened in 1980, to give today's complete run of slightly under three miles.

A fleet of varied tram types runs the line, leaving Seaton every 20 minutes during the high season. Having skirted the holiday camps, the line climbs to the level of the old railway, and the tidal estuary of the little River Axe can be seen to the right as our tramcar

swings northwards. Beyond the water lies the one-time port of Axmouth, now a quiet village. Cliffs behind and to the south, lead to the 'Elephant's Graveyard', a landslip noted for its fossil remains, and to Lyme Regis. Closer at hand, as we travel north, the river shallows abound with birdlife. As the line approaches Colyford it crosses the little River Coly, and once across the road (where the crossing was laid in bad weather over a single night) moves away from the Axe into the valley of its tributary. Road and rail converge again and the line runs into Colyton, the end of our outward journey, where a tramway shop, refreshment facility and small play area offer a pleasant place to relax awhile. The village, some ten minutes' walk away, is well worth more than a passing glance too, so there is no need whatever to take the next tram back to Seaton – unless, of course, it is the last of the day.

Shane's Castle Railway
Shane's Castle, Antrim, N Ireland, BT41 4NE.
Tel. (08494) 63380/28216

Route: Antrim – Shane's Castle
Distance: 1.5 miles
Gauge: 3 ft
Service: Variable – please enquire. Also special events.

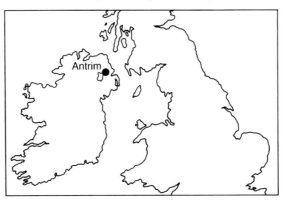

There was a 2ft gauge military line at Shane's Castle during the Second World War, a fact which may well have implanted the idea of a railway of his own in the mind of the present Lord O'Neill at an early age. It was some 20 years later however, when the preservation movement in Ireland was beginning to gain momentum, that he began to collect railway handbills, souvenirs, paintings and models: a modest display of railwayana can be seen in the workshop.

The railway opened in May 1971 and throughout its length skirts a nature reserve on the shore of Lough

Shane's Castle Railway

Neagh. A level crossing soon after the journey begins is followed by a shallow cutting and another level crossing, taking the line to the Lough side of the road. A gentle fall to Millburn Halt – a request stop, where there is a picnic site – brings the line almost to the first milepost. Beyond the subsequent bridge is a short but steep bank, which lifts the line into more open countryside. A final falling curve leads to Shane's Castle station. Though built in 1970 the station is based on a Victorian design, and features gas-lamps (now converted to electricity) from a station in Cumbria.

There are four engines on the railway. No.1 is a 0-4-0 saddle-tank named *Tyrone*, built in 1904 for the British Aluminium Company at Larne. It was bought for preservation when that Company closed in 1961, entering regular service at Shane's Castle in July 1972, where it is the principal passenger locomotive on the line. No.3 *Shane* was built as a 0-4-0 well-tank in 1949 for the Irish Turf Company, coming to this railway in June 1970: a sister engine has recently been rebuilt as a side-tank by the Talyllyn Railway. Nos 4 (1976) and 6 (*Rory* – 1974) are diesels, while No.5 *Nancy* is by some way the largest locomotive on the line. A 0-6-0 side-tank engine, she was built in Bristol in 1908 for Stanton Ironworks, working at ironstone quarries in the East Midlands until 1960. In 1972 she was acquired by the SCR, and arrived in Ireland that year, but she had previously lain in the open for ten years, and much work will be necessary before she is ready for service.

There are 12 carriages of three different types on the railway – four completely open, one completely closed, and seven with roofs but open sides. All have been built at the Estate on four-wheeled frames previously used for turf wagons. A new vehicle is expected to be in traffic in 1992. There are also three tram/trailer cars in service – the frames of these date from the early 1900s, but the bodies only from 1930. They were heavily overhauled when they arrived at Shane's Castle from Belgium in 1979.

Snaefell Mountain Railway
Laxey Station, Laxey, Isle of Man.

Route: Laxey – Snaefell Summit
Distance: 5 miles
Gauge: 3 feet 6 inches
Service: Daily 1030–1530, April – end Sept

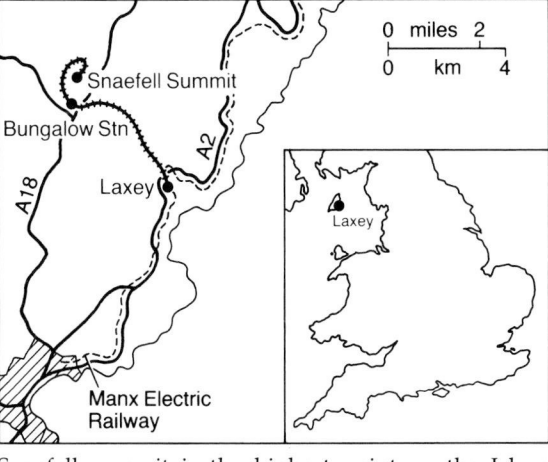

Snaefell summit is the highest point on the Isle of Man, and stands 2036 feet above sea-level. A line to the top of the mountain was proposed during the 1880s, and a route was surveyed for a steam-worked line using the Fell system of centre-rail traction. In 1893/4 however, after construction of the Manx Electric Railway (qv), it was decided that the adoption of electric power would make the Fell system unnecessary.

A different gauge was used too: though the MER was built at 3 feet, the mountain line had been planned at 3 feet 6 inches to allow for the centre-rail, and this was not changed. A temporary rail at 3 feet was laid during construction however, so that the 0-6-0 tank engine *Caledonia*, hired from the Isle of Man Railway, could assist the work. It must have been impressive on the 1 in 12 gradients! Building took only

Approaching Bungalow Station, Snaefell Mountain Railway

the very short time of seven months, between January and August 1895, and was financed by a group of Manx businessmen which then sold the railway to the Isle of Man Tramways & Electric Power Co. Ltd. At first called the Snaefell Mountain Tramway (the present title was adopted in 1903/4) the line was laid double throughout, power being supplied through overhead wires. It originally began higher up the hill than it does now, the current interchange station with the MER only opening when that Company had extended from its temporary terminus south of Glen Roy. Electricity came at first from a steam-powered generating station in the Laxey valley, but this was closed in 1924, and from 1935 current has come from the public supply.

The rolling-stock consists of six bogie-cars which date from the opening of the line.

Each seats 48 passengers. The line leaves Laxey station, climbing steeply round a shoulder of land and giving fine views of the Laxey waterwheel, below and to the right. Our car is now climbing steadily along the southern slope of Laxey Glen, reaching, after about 3.5 miles the only intermediate station. Before running

Descending from the Summit, Snaefell Mountain Railway

into it however, we cross the main Ramsey-Douglas road, part of the 'mountain' section of the Isle of Man TT course.

Beyond the station, called the Bungalow, the line curves to the right, and now it is the passengers on the left-hand side of the car who have the view, down towards Sulby Glen. The line spirals towards the summit, and after a tight curve reaches a terminus south of the summit and a few feet below it. There is no station building, but the Summit Hotel can be a welcome haven.

The views from the summit are magnificent: England lies to the east, Wales to the south. Ireland rather closer on the west. Beyond the Point of Ayre, the most northerly point of Man, are the Scottish hills of Galloway, and though you do, of course, need a clear day to see it all, the effort is well worth while.

South Tynedale Railway

Alston Railway Station, Alston, Cumbria, CA9 3JB.
Tel. (0434) 381696

Route: Alston – Gilderdale
Distance: 1.5 miles
Gauge: 2 feet
Service: Easter – October, but considerable variations. Steam at weekends and bank holidays only.

A narrow gauge railway, apparently miles from anywhere, seems an unpromising prospect, but Alston has good road access, standing roughly halfway between Darlington and Carlisle. Until 1976 it was served by a BR branch line, opened in 1852, from Haltwhistle, on the Newcastle/Carlisle line. When closure seemed to be inevitable, a preservation society

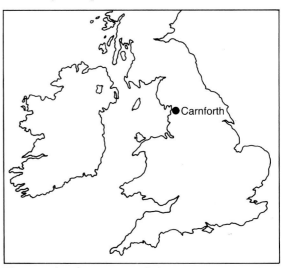
South Tynedale Railway

was formed with the idea of taking over the standard gauge branch. This project failed, and the plan was altered to a 2ft gauge line in place of the old one. Though it was to be seven years before, on 30 July 1983, the first narrow gauge train ran, things have since gone from strength to strength. In 1990 a bus-link was launched between the railway and Langwathby on the Settle & Carlisle line, connecting with trains from Lancashire and Yorkshire, and combined bus/STR tickets are available.

All but one of the steam engines are of continental origin: *Thomas Edmondson* (named after the inventor of the card-ticket), is a 0-4-0 side-tank from Spain, which entered service here in 1987. A recently commissioned Polish loco No.10 is named *NaKLÓ*, while in the workshop early in July 1991 stood *Chaka's Kraal* – built in Leeds for work in South Africa – and *Helen Kathryn*, a 0-4-0 side tank which came to the UK in 1971 and to Alston via the Bala Lake and Llanberis Lake Railways. In the station a diminuative 0-4-0 saddle-tank *Peter Pan*, had just arrived for a short stay: despite its size it had no problem with a moderately-loaded 3-coach rake. Diesels run the off-peak service, No.1 *Phoenix* bearing the brunt of this work during the early years.

Alston stands 875ft above sea level in the narrow valley where the Rivers South Tyne and Nent meet. The train is formed of modern bogie carriages custom-built for the line. In the early days of the Society passenger amenities were sparse – this new stock was introduced in 1991 and, smartly liveried in maroon and poppy, gives promise of a pleasant journey. This is northwards, following the river, which, after about half a mile, is crossed on a three-arch viaduct to take a position on the west of the valley. Maiden Way, an ancient trackway shares our route, though a little way above. This was a link between the Roman camp near Newbiggin, and Hadrian's Wall at Greenhead, via a

fort at Kirkhaugh, a little way beyond the present limit of the line.

After a mile the line reaches the site of its first terminus as a preserved railway: the half-mile extension to the present Gilderdale station opened on 13 December 1986. Beyond this point rails can be seen continuing across Gilderdale viaduct. The Society controls the trackbed to Slaggyford, a total of about five miles, but the first stage in the extension will be to Kirkhaugh, about 0.75 miles on. Members are non-committal about when it might open: '...it will depend on what volunteer labour is available,' they say. But it will surely happen.

Steamtown Miniature Railway

Warton Road, Carnforth, Lancs, LA5 9HX.
Tel. (0524) 732100

Route: North Gate – Crag Bank
Distance: 1 mile
Gauge: 15 in
Service: Most days, except 24, 25 and 26 December and 'static' days – enquire

The popular conception of the Steamtown Railway Centre at Carnforth is one of big engines – main line engines in a museum and as a servicing centre for steam specials. This is true, certainly, but Steamtown has more to offer than that, for it has a miniature railway too.

Tucked away on the western side of the site, and running for about a mile along the length of it is a line that as well as providing an enjoyable ride, gives access to the other parts of the site open to the public.

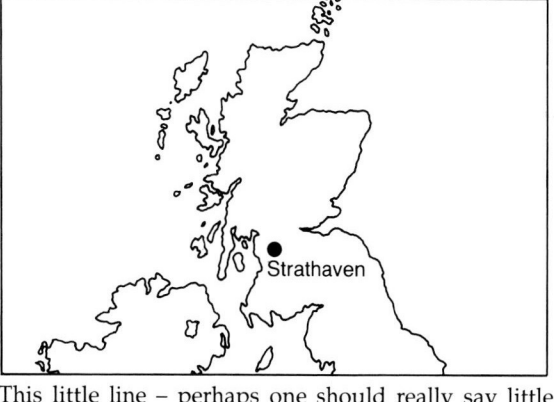

Steamtown Miniature Railway

It was opened in 1980, and begins at North Gate station, close to the main road entrance. Running southwards through the main engine shed, it emerges in the area where the main line engines are serviced, and soon reaches Steamtown Central, with, on the right, the miniature engines' shed, a water tower and Collector's Corner. Threading its way behind the carriage sidings and workshops, the next station is Green Ayre, alighting point for the Lancaster & Morecambe Model Engineers' mixed-gauge live steam layout, and last of all, Crag Bank, at the southern end of the site. Here there is a platform interchange with the standard gauge line. The line has three steam engines and two diesels. The steamers, in order of age, are *George V*, a 4-4-2 built by Henry Greenly in 1911 to a Bassett-Lowke design – it came to Carnforth via the Southport Miniature Railway. *Princess Elizabeth*, another 4-4-2, came from Southport also: she was built in 1914 and is slightly larger than *George V*, but was rebuilt in the 1930s after being almost totally destroyed by fire. She can haul four fully-laden coaches, and is a little more powerful than her fellow engine. The third steam locomotive is called *Prince William*, and was originally built to an LMS 'Black 5' 4-6-0 design in 1949. Steaming was poor however, and during the 1950s the engine was rebuilt as a 4-6-2 and is now the strongest loco on the line.

Of the diesels, *Dr. Diesel* is a diesel electric named after the inventor of the diesel engine, and was built in 1938. The engine matches *George V* in power, and is sometimes used on passenger trains in fine weather. *Royal Anchor* is a diesel hydraulic loco similar in design to BR's 'Warship' class of early diesel days. It was built in 1956 for the Liphook Railway in Hampshire, but then put in many years of sterling service not far from Carnforth, on the Ravenglass & Eskdale Railway, before coming here in 1977.

The carriages in which the visitor rides are German, thought to have been built for an exhibition in Cologne in the period between the two World Wars. Each can carry 16 passengers, and when full weighs about 1.75 tons. There is a small collection of wagons, used for maintenance of the line and for demonstration goods trains on special occasions.

Strathaven Miniature Railway

George Allen Park, Strathaven, Lanarkshire.

Route: circuits within the Park area
Distance: 1000 ft, 450 feet
Gauge: 2½, 3½, 5 and 7¼ in
Service: Easter weekend to September, w/e between 1pm and 5pm.

This little line – perhaps one should really say little lines, since there are five of them – can be found in the George Allen Park at Strathaven (pronounced Strayven), to which access is from Glasgow via East Kilbride road. It must, we think, qualify as one of the oldest miniature railways still running, having begun operations on 14 April 1949 and run continuously ever since, though there was, it must be admitted, a period in the 1970s when only an irregular service could be provided.

The original line was the brainchild of two local men, David Scott and Guy Hamilton, who laid 425 feet of 7¼-inch gauge line near the site of an old putting green in the park. They had a Greenly-built, coal-fired, 2-6-0 tender engine and three carriages, all of which, it is worth mentioning, are still in use today. The steam engine, however, failed in 1965 and was withdrawn, its place being taken by a petrol-driven locomotive. In the early 70s this too failed, but the steam engine was restored in 1977. By the end of the decade though, the line, previously run by the Avondale Modelling Club, needed new track.

Renaming itself the Strathaven Model Society, the Club undertook to refurbish and provide this, and has indeed supplied much more, for the site now sports no less than four different gauges on two different routes. There is a section at ground level with 7¼ and 5-inch gauge track, about 1000 feet in length, with steaming bays and a traverser. There is also a raised section which uses the site of the original line, having gauges of 2½, 3½ and 5 inches, and this has a running length of about 450 feet, together with steaming bays and a turntable.

As well as running all the services, the Strathaven Model Society is responsible for maintenance of the two layouts. Open days during the season have sometimes attracted as many as 20 different locomotives from visiting members of local modelling societies. Many tourists visit the site also, and, says James Brattey, Treasurer of the Club: '...we can expect to carry over 16,000 passengers in one season.'

There were great celebrations on the 40th birthday, of course, when 23 September 1989 was nominated as a special event day. The original steam locomotive underwent a major overhaul at a cost of about £2000, and a further £500 was invested in new carriages including automatic braking equipment to enhance public safety. Let us hope that Strathaven's 'wee train' is still steaming strong when it reaches its golden jubilee.

Strathaven Miniature Railway

Teifi Valley Railway

Station Yard, Henllan, Llandyssul, Dyfed, SA44 5HX. Tel. (0559) 371077

Route: Henllan – Pontprenshitw
Distance: 1.25 miles
Gauge: 2 feet
Service: Daily, Easter – mid-October.

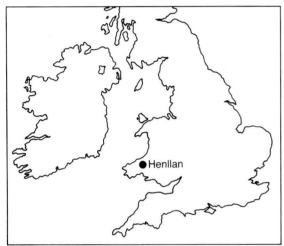

The Carmarthen & Cardigan Railway was here first, with a projected broad gauge (7ft 0¼in) line aimed at linking the South Wales Railway at Carmarthen with the coast. By the time it reached Newcastle Emlyn (it got no further) in 1895 the broad gauge had been abolished in South Wales for 23 years, so it was on the standard gauge that a passenger service survived until 1952. Goods lasted another 23 years, but before a local preservation society was able to do anything about saving the line, overgrowth was rampant. A base was established at Henllan, the first station east of Newcastle Emlyn, and during the winter of 1984 a little progress was made in adverse conditions. A mile was cleared by the next Spring, and stone from the old platform was moved 200yd westwards to make a new one. Tracklaying began then, and the first section of line opened on 24 August 1985, and its distance was doubled with the opening of an extension to Pontprenshitw. Since then a further 1000yd has come into service, and the eventual aim, to run a six-mile line from Newcastle Emlyn to Llandyssul is slowly taking shape.

The line, beginning at Henllan, runs in a shallow cutting at first, and then on to a high embankment. A nature trail has been laid out in ancient woodland here, to the north of the line, and is served by a

Teifi Valley Railway

'request' halt. Beyond, a small bridge leads on to a rocky ledge above the River Teifi, which runs far below on the southern side. The line begins to fall now, and runs into Pont-prenshitw, a new station built on a quarry site. Paths lead down to the river from here, to give a view of the bridge 80ft above, a sturdy stone structure which replaced the pont (bridge) pren (wooden) shitw (shaky) that was there before the railway came. A 10-minute stop is made here during return journeys, so that passengers may walk to see the bridge if they wish.

Alan George was the first steam engine on the line, a 0-4-0 saddle-tank built in 1894, and a brother locomotive to *Lilian* (see Launceston Steam Railway) from Penrhyn Quarry. Though in working order when bought in 1983, overhaul was needed and was completed by 1986. There are four diesels on the roster, though one of these is not yet in working order. Carriage stock is home-made – it was designed by a member of the preservation society and built on site at Henllan. Carriage No.1 is a passenger/guard composite, No.2 has wide doors for wheelchair passengers, No.3 is a saloon and No.4 is under construction. The wagon stock is used for maintenance – dumper wagons have been bought, and two bolster wagons were built at Henllan.

One of the most important areas connected with this line is the nature trail already mentioned, with which there has been incorporated a campfire site with a terraced amphitheatre seating 200. Thousands of hours of backbreaking manual work have paid off (there is no mechanical access to the area), and details of the flora and fauna to be seen are obtainable at Henllan station.

Vale of Rheidol Light Railway

c/o Brecon Mountain Railway, Pant Station, Mid-Glamorgan, CF48 2UP.

Route: Aberystwyth – Devil's Bridge
Distance: 11.5 miles
Gauge: 1 ft 11½ in
Service: End-March – end-September.

In 1902 a narrow gauge railway of 1ft 11.5in was opened, built between Aberystwyth on the Welsh coast and a beauty spot a few yards under 12 miles inland called Devil's Bridge. The prime object was to serve leadmines and timber slopes in the valley, though there is no doubt that the promoters of the line had an eye to the tourist potential also. It was completed just within the period allowed by its Light Railway Order, but the lead traffic soon waned, a shortfall which was not made up by the timber trade. After ten years a decision was made to concentrate on the tourists, and in 1913 the Company amalgamated with the Cambrian Railways. The Cambrian however did little to liven things up, and when that Company was itself taken over by the GWR as part of the 1923 Grouping, the VoR of course came too. The new owner scrapped two of the old engines, built two new ones and rebuilt *Prince of Wales*, and virtually rebuilt the line too. Goods trains ceased in the mid-1920s, and the line closed during World War Two. After Nationalisation, passenger figures rose from 34,000 in 1954 to 179,500 in 1975, but five years later had fallen just below 112,000. In 1987, amid a good deal of controversy, BR sold the concern to the Brecon Mountain Railway, which now runs it, though the new owners admit that it is going to take time to refurbish, as they would wish to, an asset that had been somewhat rundown.

For many years VoR trains used to leave Aberysytwyth in a southward direction from the car park/stock market beside the BR station. Then, having crossed beneath the standard gauge Carmarthen branch, they would loop back behind the engine shed before proceeding towards the hills. Passenger trains now leave from the old Carmarthen line platform of the BR station, passing directly behind the old standard gauge steam shed, now with narrow gauge rails laid through it. At Llanbadarn, on the outskirts of Aberystwyth, the line crosses a road on the level and a long trestle bridge, one of the more costly matters needing attention. In another three miles the train reaches Capel Bangor, marked by little other than an open level crossing, after which climbing begins though not yet too steeply. Nantyronen, at 7.5 miles

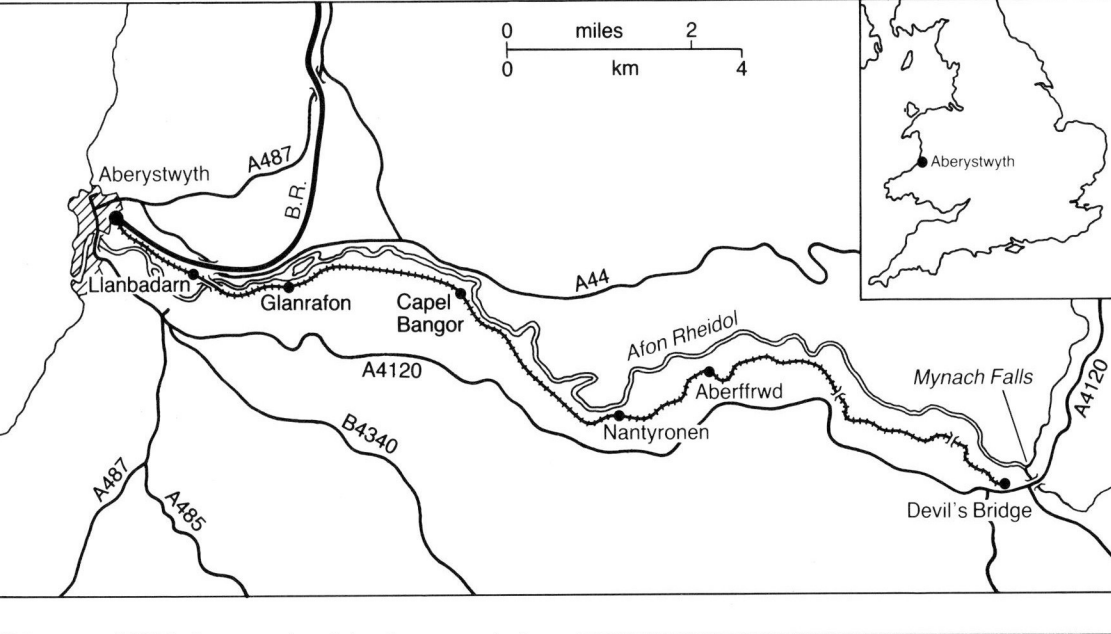

No. 9, 'Prince of Wales', at Devil's Bridge Station

distance and 220ft above sea level, has been a watering point in recent years. Beyond the station the line reaches the ruling grade of 1 in 50: though level stretches ease the climb to begin with, there is much more climbing to follow as the line penetrates the upper valley.

Aberffrwd (8 miles, 280ft, and pronounced Aberfrood) has been restored to its original role of crossing point after 17 years of demotion, and the gradient is continuous at 1 in 50 from 200 yards east of the station, with numerous sharp curves. At last, after a final curve and a rock-cutting, Devil's Bridge is gained and at last the gradient eases, the line having climbed 400ft in the four miles from Aberffrwd. It is just possible to follow a train up the valley by car, meeting it at most of the road-crossings, but it is necessary to know precisely where to go, and in narrow lanes where a tractor or caravan might be met at almost any point, is not recommended. Devil's Bridge has a refreshment room and shop, but very little shelter in a downpour. The falls themselves, the objectives of most passengers, lie a short walk down the road, and are a rewarding if somewhat exhausting excursion.

Three locomotives work the line, all 2-6-2 side-tank engines, which, in 1978-80 were converted to oil-firing. Though they overhang for 3ft on each side of the track, both they and the carriages are remarkably steady. No.9 *Prince of Wales* was built in 1902 by Davies & Metcalfe, and extensively rebuilt by the

Devil's Bridge Station, Vale of Rheidol Light Railway

No. 9, 'Prince of Wales', approaching Devil's Bridge Station, Vale of Rheidol Light Railway

GWR at Swindon in 1924. No.7 *Owain Glyndwr*, No.8 *Llywelyn* were both new engines built at Swindon in 1923, whose engineers closely followed the original Davies & Metcalfe design of 1902. After the BMR takeover, No.9 spent some while at Pant, undergoing a heavy overhaul in that Company's works: it is now back on duty and it is intended to deal with the others similarly as time and money allow, No.7 being the next in line. Locomotive liveries have varied considerably over the years, No.9 appearing in original VoR ochre followed by BR blue with arrows, No.8 in BR blue followed by Cambrian black, and No.7 in blue, then BR Brunswick green with lining. No.9 emerged from the Pant workshops in red, but so far as the others are concerned, only time will tell.

The present carriage stock was supplied new by the GWR in 1938, after most of the originals had been scrapped. Some vehicles are open, but there are closed ones too, in deference no doubt to Welsh rain, which for some strange reason has always seemed to this writer much better than that which falls anywhere else! All vehicles have glazed ends – after all, this is arguably one of the most scenic lines in Wales – metal sides with mesh to waist height and canvas screens for use in bad weather. Seats are reversible, and each carriage will seat 48 passengers.

Walsall Arboretum Railway

Arboretum Park Extension, Broadway Ring Road, Walsall ˮˮ   nds.

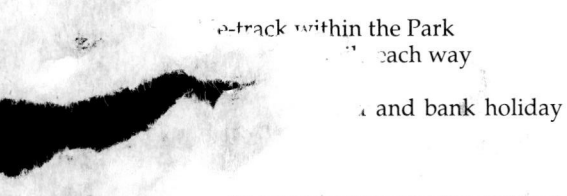

... e-track within the Park

... each way

... and bank holiday

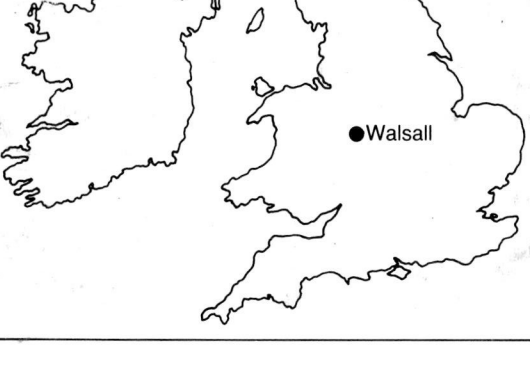

This little line is something rather different. It is owned by Walsall Leisure Services, and runs along the northern edge of Walsall's Arboretum Extension, for the most part in a pleasantly shady avenue of trees for a distance of about half a mile. Since it is double-tracked throughout, this means a mile of railway, without any curve of note.

At one end it runs from a platform near the bathing/paddling pool, an extremely popular venue on a hot afternoon. The platform road here has been built up to give a level run: considerably lower at first, it was found that the motive power was having trouble in starting on the gradient. The turntable has been left where it was however, so that trains running into the terminus must now be detached from the engine before reaching the platform. The locomotive then makes two reversals to reach the slope to the turntable, and once it is clear the coaches are hand-shunted into the platform.

At the other end of the line is the workshop. The line is laid with aluminium rail, much easier to handle than other metals, though it does create difficulties when constructing pointwork. Fares are deliberately set low, and an enjoyably relaxed atmosphere surrounds the line. Not that any of the important things – safety, for instance – are treated casually – only one train at a time is allowed on any track, and this two-train operation means a roughly ten-minute interval service in each direction.

Richard Wall, who is responsible for providing a service along the line, is in regular contact with a group of locomotive owners who are only too happy, as a rule, to bring their engines for a day's running when they can. The line is popular with them because, being straight and level, it allows them to use the railway as a testing and running-in ground – this also means that there is a continual variety of motive power on the line, a factor which is much liked by the

customers. And since this also means that Richard can now and then use some of the tramcar models he builds himself, everyone is happy.

On a typical Sunday afternoon a model Class 35 Hymek diesel, powered by an electric generator, might be under test, while the locomotive providing steam interest for the afternoon could be a superb model of a Great Western 2-6-2 tank engine. Each hauls three 'sit-astride' vehicles which seat four passengers apiece. Beyond the platform at the workshop end of the line is a spur of track leading away on a curve to the right beside the turntable. It does not go far.

'We have authority to build a branch along there,' says Richard, 'but security is a problem, so the final decision hasn't yet been made'.

Perhaps by the time you get there it will be done.

Welsh Highland Railway

Porthmadog, Gwynedd, LL49 9DY. Tel. (0766) 513402: out of season (051 608) 1950 (day), (051 327) 3576 (eve).

Route: Porthmadog – Pen-y-Mount
Distance: 0.75 miles
Gauge: 1 ft 11½ in
Service: Easter – end-October

In 1923 the Welsh Highland Railway (22 miles) was the longest narrow gauge line in Wales. From Porthmadog, on the northern shore of Cardigan Bay, it ran through the pass of Aberglaslyn to Beddgelert. It then crossed the lower slopes of Snowdon before ending its journey at Dinas Junction on the standard gauge line from Afon Wen to Caernarvon. Between Porthmadog and Beddgelert it was joined by a horse-worked tramway from slate mines in the Croesor valley, and there were slate quarries at the other end too, near Bryngwyn. Were it open to this extent today it would no doubt be a successful line, but between the Wars tourism was not such big business as now, and in 1937 the line closed, having run at a loss for years. Stock was sold in 1940, track lifted in 1941, no doubt aiding the War effort, and much of the trackbed reverted to vegetation.

In 1964 a group of people decided that the line was worth reviving. The trackbed belonged to the Official Receiver, and other than this there was nothing left. In 1976 the site of an old slate exchange siding beside BR's Porthmadog station was bought, and nearby Gelert's farm was bought three years later. Slowly track was laid, rolling stock built and locomotives acquired. A summer service has run since 1980.

The line, for all its present shortness, can boast no fewer than five steam engines and eight diesels. Of the steamers three are in working order. *Russell*, a 2-6-2 side-tank engine, was built in 1906 for the North Wales Narrow Gauge Railway, passing to the WHR in 1923. After many adventures it returned to service on the WHR in 1987, now splendidly rebuilt. *Karen* dates from 1942, built for the Selukwe Peak Light Railway,

belonging to the Rhodesia Chrome Mines Ltd. She is a 0-4-2 side-tank, and after restoration became, in 1983, the first steam engine to run on the newly relaid line. In August 1991 the 0-4-2 side-tank *Gelert*, became the third working steam loco in the fleet – built for service in South Africa, she is capable of hauling heavy trains to Beddgelert when the time comes. The other steam engines await attention: *Kinnerley* and *Glaslyn* are diesels, from 1953 and 1952 respectively. These are the only two equipped to work passenger trains – the other serviceable engines work maintenance trains and wait to help build the extension.

Passengers on the WHR will find a variety of stock, much of it built at Gelert's Farm, but the pride of the line must be the original NWNG carriage known as the 'Gladstone' coach, once; so legend has it, used by the great man. This was recovered from a Harlech garden after 40 years' use as a shed, and is now being rebuilt to enter service late in 1992. The former WHR buffet car has also been rescued and awaits restoration. Beyond the farm the mountains of Snowdonia act as a powerful lure, and remain the ultimate goal of the railway.

Welsh Highland Railway